W9-CKC-498

ACCORDING
to Your
MERCY

ACCORDING to Your MERCY

*Praying with the Psalms
from Ash Wednesday to Easter*

MARTIN SHANNON, CJ

PARACLETE PRESS
BREWSTER, MASSACHUSETTS

2017 First Printing

According to Your Mercy: Praying with the Psalms from Ash Wednesday to Easter

Copyright © 2017 by Rev. Robert Shannon

ISBN 978-1-61261-773-2

Scripture quotations, unless otherwise noted, are from the Revised Standard Version of the Bible, copyright 1952 [2nd edition, 1971] by the Division of Christian Education of the National Council of the Churches of Christ in the United States of America. Used by permission. All rights reserved.

Scripture quotations designated NRSV are taken from the New Revised Standard Version of the Bible, copyright 1989, Division of Christian Education of the National Council of the Churches of Christ in the United States of America. Used by permission. All rights reserved.

All quotations from the Daily Office Lectionary of the Book of Common Prayer (BCP) as adopted by the General Convention of 1928 and amended by subsequent Conventions.

The Paraclete Press name and logo (dove on cross) are trademarks of Paraclete Press, Inc.

Library of Congress Cataloging-in-Publication Data
    Names: Shannon, Martin, author.
    Title: According to your mercy : praying with the Psalms from Ash Wednesday
        to Easter / Martin Shannon, CJ.
    Description: Brewster, MA : Paraclete Press Inc., [2017] | Includes
        bibliographical references.
    Identifiers: LCCN 2016051094 | ISBN 9781612617732 (trade paper)
    Subjects: LCSH: Bible. Psalms--Devotional use. | Lent--Prayers and devotions.
    Classification: LCC BS1430.54 .S53 2017 | DDC 242/.34--dc23
    LC record available at https://lccn.loc.gov/2016051094

10 9 8 7 6 5 4 3 2 1

All rights reserved. No portion of this book may be reproduced, stored in an electronic retrieval system, or transmitted in any form or by any means—electronic, mechanical, photocopy, recording, or any other—except for brief quotations in printed reviews, without prior permission of the publisher.

Published by Paraclete Press
Brewster, Massachusetts
www.paracletepress.com
Printed in the United States of America

*Answer me, O L*ORD, *for thy steadfast love is good;*
according to thy abundant mercy, turn to me.
Psalm 69:16

CONTENTS

Introduction

WE PRAY THE PSALMS ALMOST EVERY DAY IN MY community: morning, midday, and evening. In four weeks' time we sing through the entire Psalter, and then we start again. You might expect that after years of such rhythmic repetition, the psalms would lose their freshness and certainly their capacity to surprise. But our experience, and the experience of generations before us, tells us quite the opposite. Since the time of ancient Israel and long before Christians adopted the Psalter as their own prayer book, the psalms have been an inexhaustible source of inspiration, a limitless cache of words, phrases, and images for truth-filled worship. Why? Because, before all else, the psalms are *prayers*, and there is no sell-by date on the heart's language of prayer.

I have written elsewhere that the language of the psalms is the language of the kingdom of God. In many respects for us it is a foreign language, or at least an unfamiliar one. We aren't used to addressing God quite so directly, so vulnerably, so candidly. As poetry, this language requires us to stretch our imaginations, step outside of ourselves, and listen carefully to the psalmist's heart. In such listening, we often hear the prayerful beat of our own heart and find ourselves saying, "I know exactly what the psalmist means here."

In Hebrew, this poetry is intensely compact, capable of bearing multiple meanings in a single line. Its structure is well-ordered and highly intentional, factors that sometimes are not evident when rendered in English. Nevertheless, even if we do not grasp the meaning, we can tell where the words are taking us. Sometimes, the prayer poems take us to lofty heights of adoration and gladness—O *sing to the* LORD *a new song, for he has done marvelous things!* (Ps. 98:1). At other times, deep into the dark recesses of the human heart—*May [my enemy's] children be fatherless, and his wife a widow!* (109:9). And sometimes the words fairly crack with hope—*Whither shall I go from thy Spirit? Or whither shall I flee from thy presence?* (139:7)—or with ache—*Out of the depths I cry to thee, O* LORD! (130:1). At all times, however, the psalms give us a vocabulary for bringing our true selves before God. They school us in the art of prayerful candor, for the psalms say what is true—about ourselves and about God.

Sometime in the fourth century, a certain deacon fell ill and decided to spend some of his convalescence studying the psalms. He wrote a letter to his bishop and friend, Athanasius of Alexandria, asking for guidance and insight. He received back more than he had bargained for, as he had tapped into his bishop's deep love of the Psalter. Athanasius answered: The psalms are like a mirror in which any reader can see reflected all the varied emotions and thoughts of his or her own heart. Better yet, they are like a lavish garden from which may be cut a fruitful prayer for any and every condition of life. "For," he wrote, "I believe that the whole of human existence, both the dispositions of the soul and the movements of the thoughts, have been measured out and encompassed in those very words of the Psalter."[1] No wonder, more than a thousand years later, the great church reformer John Calvin liked to call the book of Psalms "the anatomy of all the parts of the human soul."[2]

At the Community of Jesus, after we gather for Morning Prayer—Lauds (from the Latin for "praise")—we spend fifteen minutes in private prayer and reading before gathering again to celebrate Eucharist. The reflections collected in this book were written originally as a daily guide for that time of silent prayer. Often, the psalm was taken from that particular morning's liturgy, allowing us a bit more time to gaze into the "mirror" of the psalmist's prayer and to make it our own.

This book contains forty-seven such reflections, one for each of the days from Ash Wednesday to Easter. For the most part, at least until Palm Sunday, they are not organized in any particular order. They are simply a collection of prayers that reflect various twists and turns on the Lenten journey. As a season of preparation and penitence, Lent lends itself well to such meandering for, when all is said and done, we know where we will end up.

Like Athanasius, many of the church fathers preached and wrote about the psalms, and a quotation from one of their works is also offered each day, as another way to "look into" the psalm. And, because the purpose of both the psalm and the comments is to lead us to prayer, I offer a prayer of my own, written during those *lectio* times between Lauds and Eucharist. Better still, of course, would be for the reader (the *pray*-er) to compose her or his own.

In his *Confessions*, St. Augustine wrote of his delight at hearing the psalms chanted in church. But, he cautioned, listening is not the same as praying. You must learn to use the words in your conversation with God—if not to express your own thoughts and emotions, then to express the praise and the pain of others for whom we pray. By providing him with true language, wrote

Augustine, these prayers set his faith on fire and roused in him a voice with which to proclaim the glory of God. The prayers of the psalms taught him the prayer of his own heart. *According to Your Mercy* is offered as one classroom among many in the school of prayer that we call the Psalter.

REFLECTIONS

1

Ash Wednesday
PSALM 121

My help comes from the LORD,
who made heaven and earth.

v. 2

THE COLLECTION OF PSALMS FROM 120 THROUGH 134, each of which is entitled "A Song of Ascents," is thought to have formed a small prayer book for pilgrims making their way to Jerusalem to celebrate one of the annual Jewish festivals in the temple. Psalm 121 could be the words of a pilgrim making the sometimes dangerous journey through the Judean wilderness on his "way up" to the Holy City. The author is in the company of fellow pilgrims and, as the day ends and the night's darkness creeps into the valley, the troop of travelers assigns watchmen to climb the surrounding hillsides and stand guard over the encampment. Predatory bands of thieves in that region know the timetable of seasonal meetings at the temple. The pilgrims' only hope for protection is the watchful eyes and warning voices of their guardian keepers.

Perhaps the hills reminded the poet of the story of Elisha and his angelic defenders. The Syrian army had come by stealth at night and surrounded him. *Don't be afraid*, said Elisha to his trembling servant, *for those who are with us are more than those who are with them.* Then the Lord opened the eyes of the young man, and he saw: "Behold, the mountain was full of horses and chariots of fire round about Elisha" (2 Kgs. 6:17). The psalmist also saw help in the hills.

I will lift up mine eyes unto the hills, whispers the pilgrim as he prepares to enter his tent for the night. He sees the appointed watchmen, but, he asks himself, *Is that where my help truly comes from? No,* he quickly replies, as if to the stars in the sky. *There is Another whom I cannot see, but I know that he is there, keeping watch. He has been with us all day, and he will never leave us through the night. Those who would do us harm are not the only ones who know our goings and comings. The Lord himself looks over us and he will be our help. The hills are filled with his presence, for he stands ever-alert beside each of our watchmen. Even if the travels of the day weary them to unwilling sleep, he who made heaven and earth will never slumber. His sleepless eyes will never be closed to us. His unblinking gaze will never wander from us. Knowing, then, that it is the Lord who keeps us, I will lie down now, and sleep in peace* (see Ps. 4:8).

FROM THE FATHERS

"May the Lord protect your coming in and your going out." Now look at the "coming out" of the furnace and the "going in" to it: "Count it all joy, my brethren, when you meet various trials" (James 1:2). There you are—it is easy enough to go in; coming out is the big thing. But do not worry: "God is faithful"—because you have gone in, you are naturally thinking about getting out— "God is faithful, and he will not let you be tempted beyond your strength, but with the temptation will also provide the way out"

(1 Cor. 10:13). What is the way out? "That you may be able to endure." You have gone in, you have fallen in; you have endured, you have come out.

Augustine

Today, I begin walking with you to Jerusalem, Lord,
 to a place of death . . . and of life.
Along the way—here in the wilderness,
 also a place of death . . . and of life—
I will go out with you,
 and I will come in with you.
If you will only keep me.

2

Thursday before Lent I
PSALM 99

Extol the LORD our God, and worship at his holy mountain;
for the LORD our God is holy!

v. 9

WHILE MANY PSALMS OF PRAISE EMPHASIZE THE call for "*all* the earth" to worship the Lord, Psalm 99 focuses upon the particular people who are called by his name. While including "all the peoples" (Ps. 99:2) as the subjects of God's eternal reign, the psalmist quickly narrows his focus to those, including himself, who address the Lord as *our* God (verses 5, 8, 9). These are the people who would be most familiar with the language he uses and the references he makes:

- the cherubim: the golden figures hovering over the ark of the covenant (Exod. 25:18)
- Zion: the chosen dwelling place of the Most High (Ps. 132:13)
- Jacob: the twelve tribes, therefore the entire family of the covenant
- God's footstool: the temple and particularly the ark (1 Chr. 28:2)

- Moses, Aaron, and Samuel: representing the sacred triad of the covenant: the law, the priesthood, and the prophets
- the cloudy pillar: God's guiding presence as he led the children of Israel through the wilderness
- God's holy hill: Jerusalem, the city of God

There is a concentration of meaning in these short verses that makes an unmistakable impression—*all* peoples are called upon to praise the Lord, but above all the people whom God calls his own, the people who have experienced firsthand his power and mercy. These are the people whom God delivered from oppression and slavery; who followed God's guiding hand through the wilderness; who heard God's voice through his appointed prophets and priests; who knew both the forgiving and the disciplining love of God. No other people to that point had been treated by God with such attention or such favor (see Ps. 147:20).

Three times the psalmist says God is holy; this is the summary declaration of the entire psalm (Ps. 99:3, 5, 9). The psalms tell us again and again that praise has everything to do with God and nothing to do with us, except insofar as we are chosen by God and loved by God. Praise is *always* appropriate because God is *always* holy, *always* Lord, *always* God.

FROM THE FATHERS

[Do not think that] when this life comes to an end, that is the end for us of God's praises. Not at all; we shall praise him then much more, when we are living without end. If we praise him during the exile we are passing through, how, do you think, shall we praise him at the home we are never to leave? . . . Living the blessed life in which God is to be perceived without any uncertainty, to be loved without any weariness, to be praised without end, why, yes indeed, that will be what our being alive consists of—seeing, loving, praising God.

Augustine

I am among those you have called, Lord,
    those you have saved, those you have forgiven,
        —and, yes, sometimes reprimanded—
    those you have always loved.
I am one of "your people." (This is a marvel to me.)
I am among those who will praise you today . . .
    those who will always praise you.

3

Friday before Lent I
PSALM 132

I will not give sleep to my eyes or slumber to my eyelids,
until I find a place for the LORD,
a dwelling place for the Mighty One of Jacob.

vv. 4–5

Psalm 132 is another of the "Songs of Ascent," which comprise a unique section of the book of Psalms. It focuses on the Lord's temple in Jerusalem and recalls the events of 2 Samuel 7, when David's desire to build a house for God is transformed into God's promise to build a kingdom founded upon the house of David. It is said that you can never out-give God, and this event is most certainly a prime example.

It may be that this psalm is associated with an annual remembrance of the dedication of the temple, a kind of reenactment of the "conversation" between David and God that eventually led to the building of the temple by Solomon. As such, it is not surprising to find it among those songs sung by pilgrims as they approached the Holy City at times of festival.

On a more personal level, the psalm has something to say about the two sides of any agreement, especially any agreement between

God and one of his people. The first half of the psalm emphasizes David's side of the contract. He is the "I" of verses 3 through 5. The psalmist recalls David's dedication to the self-imposed task of building "a dwelling place for the Mighty One of Jacob." In the end, it doesn't matter at all that it is not to be David's hands that build the temple. What is being stressed is the depth of his desire to do so, a desire so strong that he promised to allow himself no rest until the task was accomplished. It is because of the strength of David's intention that the temple comes to be built. "Lord, remember David."

The second half of the psalm describes how David's promise to God, as generous as it is, is surpassed by God's own promise to David. The "I" of verses 11 through 18 is the Lord. What does God promise? That he, too, intends to build a house for himself, a dwelling place where he will "rest" and "have a delight." So while David is speaking of a place, God is speaking of a people. The house in which he promises to live has the Son of David as its cornerstone, "in whom the whole structure is joined together and grows into a holy temple in the Lord" (Eph. 2:22 NRSV).

FROM THE FATHERS

Who would not be amazed at such a love of God, such dedication of soul, that a king and prophet should deny himself all sleep— the very essential of bodily vigor—until he should find a place to build a temple to the Lord? This fact should be a strong admonishment to us who long to be a dwelling place of the Lord and to be considered his tabernacle and temple forever. "You are," as Paul reminds us, "the temple of the living God" (1 Cor. 3:16). Let us, then, be moved by the example of the saints to love vigils to the utmost of our power.

Nicetas of Remesiana

David's prayer is filled with such passion, Lord,
such dedication, such undeterred commitment.
His plan is in place, and he will not be thwarted,
until he meets with your plan—your commitment, your passion.
No question who will win that contest.
Here are my plans today . . . and here are yours.
Any question who will win this contest?

4

Saturday before Lent I
PSALM 1

His delight is in the law of the LORD,
and on his law he meditates day and night.

v. 2

RONT DOORS CAN TELL US A LOT ABOUT THE DWELLING places that lie behind them, and maybe something about the people who dwell there as well. Architects put serious thought into the way a building is "presented" by its main entrance, carefully choosing its size, shape, material, color, and even lighting, for the sake of both the door's practical purposes and its symbolic significance. We will probably never know how this psalm became the opening psalm—the "front door"—for the entire Psalter, but we can be sure that the choice was not made arbitrarily. For centuries, commentators have seen Psalm 1 as an intentionally placed doorway leading to the 149 psalms that follow. Origen considered it to be not only a doorway but also a pithy summary of the meaning of all the psalms.

What is it about this psalm that lends itself to this extraordinary role? In six short verses, using a few simple images, Psalm 1 tells us succinctly that living for God results in eternal happiness, while living apart from God results in utter extinction. One cannot find two more diametrically opposed outcomes to human existence. Consider the following:

- The opening word of the psalm, *ashrei* (happy, or blessed), describes the hope of every human heart. It communicates a sense of deep longing and active pursuit. Note also that this first word of the psalm begins with the first letter of the Hebrew alphabet, *aleph*, while the last word of the psalm—*toveid* (perish)—begins with the last letter of the Hebrew alphabet, *tav*. Two opposite states, blessedness and death, result from choices, and those choices could not be further apart.

- The word *law* here is the Hebrew word *torah*, which has less to do with rules and restrictions than it has to do with teachings and directions. *Torah* describes God's ways and purposes: the directions he gives so that we can walk beside him, and the things he tells us about himself so that we can get to know him. The one who meditates on *torah*, who "chews over" God's ways, will be known by God forever.

- The "tree" in verse 3, which stands securely and fruitfully by the river, appears in some manuscripts as the "tree of life." What a remarkable thing! If we'd been patient—if we'd honored *torah* from the very beginning—we could have eaten of the tree of life all along. Our life in Paradise begins here and now, with our walking, standing, and sitting—day and night—in the good company of the Lord.

FROM THE FATHERS

Like the foundation in a house, the keel in a ship, and the heart in a body, so is [Psalm 1 as a] brief introduction to the whole structure of the Psalms. For when David intended to propose . . . to the combatants of true religion the many painful tasks involving unmeasured sweats and toils, he showed first the happy end, that in the hope of the blessings reserved for us, we might endure without grief the sufferings of this life.

Basil the Great

Today, like every day, I will be confronted with choices, Lord.
Where I walked and stood and sat yesterday,
     and the day before . . . and the day before that,
   will help or hinder me today.
So today—where I walk, and stand, and sit—
   will help or hinder me tomorrow.
Today, like every day, I will be confronted with choices, Lord.

5

First Sunday of Lent
PSALM 2

"You are my son, today I have begotten you.
Ask of me, and I will make the nations your heritage,
and the ends of the earth your possession."
vv. 7–8

I F PSALM 1 IS THE DOORWAY INTO THE PSALTER, PSALM 2 is the vestibule. Put together, these two psalms locate our longed-for state of peace and happiness in the ways of God and in the sovereignty of God. The man or woman whose life is blessed by delighting in God's law (Ps. 1:2) is the same man or woman who is blessed for taking refuge in God (2:11). Whoever compiled these songs of prayer and praise, no doubt under the inspiration of the Holy Spirit, paired these two opening psalms quite intentionally. It's almost as if the second takes up where the first leaves off: "The way of the wicked will perish." "Why do . . . the peoples plot in vain?" In Psalm 1, God's ways and man's ways are set in clear opposition to one another, and Psalm 2 declares the inevitable winner.

It is likely that this psalm was written and appointed for use at the coronation of a king in the line of David. Many of the same themes that appear elsewhere in connection with David's own anointing and the divine promises made to his descendants appear among these lines: the unbreakable bond between the Lord and his anointed (Ps. 2:2); God's personal appointment of Israel's king (6); likening the king to God's own son (7); and the rule of Israel's king being honored by all the nations of the world (10). Woven through the entire song is the unmistakable melody of God's sovereign rule over the whole earth and all of its peoples. To illustrate this, the psalmist presents perhaps the most anthropomorphic picture of Yahweh to appear in all of the psalms: God *laughing* at those who conspire against him (4)! He is utterly undisturbed by the schemes, conniving, resistance, and outright rebellion that are part of the human condition. Nothing whatsoever can change this indisputable fact: the Lord is God.

No wonder the first Christians found such inspiration and reassurance in the message of Psalm 2. When Peter and John were released from prison—for preaching and healing in the name of Jesus—they found their friends and told them what had happened. After years of reciting Psalm 2 in the synagogue, they surely knew the words by heart, for Luke tells us that they lifted up their voices and said the psalm together. For them, the anointed son spoken of by the psalmist was Jesus; the raging nations were Herod and Pontius Pilate; and the irresistible rod of God was the power to heal and work wonders in the name of Jesus Christ (see Acts 4:23–31). Even the schemes of hell broke apart upon the rock of Christ. How much more will human resistance—*our* resistance—crumble before his sovereign rule.

FROM THE FATHERS

[The words of the psalm] come from someone deploring and censuring folly. . . . Despite their conspiring together and hatching a tawdry plot for the murder of the Lord, their schemes all came to nothing, as they were unable to consign to oblivion the one crucified by them: on the third day he rose again and took possession of the world.

Theodoret of Cyr

Father, my resistance to you takes many forms—
　　some of them I don't even recognize.
Still, I am among your Son's most prized possessions.
Why, then, should I not laugh, too—why should I not laugh with you—
　　at my foolishness?

6

Monday of Lent I
PSALM 11

In the LORD I take refuge.

v. 1

"THE LORD IS IN HIS HOLY TEMPLE, THE LORD'S throne is in heaven" (Ps. 11:4). Psalm 11 is arranged around this simple statement. It is a statement of faith, of course, because the psalmist cannot actually "see" God enthroned in heaven. He does not yet see with his own eyes the divine glory of the Lord. What he actually does see, however, is cause for the poet to be worried. The ungodly—those who neither know nor care to know the ways of God—seem to surround him. Their attacks are like so many flying arrows, aimed with malice at the righteous. They are intent upon the destruction of those who, like birds, are utterly defenseless against such ruthlessness.

Some suggest to the psalmist that he fly away "to the hill" to find refuge. The image is of a flittering sparrow, leaping from its tree branch and flying from place to place in search of escape. But the "hill" to which the psalmist refers is a false sanctuary. In the language of the psalms, the hills, in addition to Mount Zion, often refer to the places where false gods are worshiped. For example,

Psalm 121 opens with the question: "I lift up my eyes to the hills. From whence does my help come?" He may be looking to "God's dwelling place" for help, or he may be saying: *In the midst of trouble, can I expect help from the gods of those hills? No, for "my help comes from the* LORD, *who made heaven and earth"* (Ps. 121:2).

With the uncertainty and fear the psalmist describes, it is easy to discount his affirmation of faith in God's sovereignty as so much wishful thinking. "Everything will work out alright" is regularly offered as an easy assurance in times of distress. Though this message may be true, it is without foundation unless it is based upon a deeper truth: *God reigns supreme. There is no stronger power, no surer footing, no securer refuge than the Lord himself. Though all else may change, this single fact remains certain. The mountain may seem to be a safe place. But God is the only "hill" able to offer true and lasting shelter.*

FROM THE FATHERS

Great is the power of hope in the Lord, invincible citadel, unassailable rampart, insuperable reinforcement, tranquil haven, impregnable power, irresistible weapon, unconquerable strength, capable of making a refuge where none seems possible. . . . I have the Lord of the universe as my ally. The one who, without difficulty, created everything everywhere is my leader and support, and you would send me to the wilderness to seek my safety in the desert? After all, surely the help from the desert cannot surpass the One who is capable of doing *anything* with complete ease.

John Chrysostom

You know better than anyone, Father,

certainly better than me,

the things and people and places where I look for safety.

You also know better than anyone,

and definitely better than I do,

that there is no safe place for me

outside the walls of your temple,

outside the protection of your embrace.

If I am going to flee anywhere today,

and I will certainly flee somewhere,

let it be to you.

7

Tuesday of Lent I
PSALM 7

O let the evil of the wicked come to an end,
but establish thou the righteous,
thou who triest the minds and hearts, thou righteous God.

v. 9

CCUSATION IS A PAINFUL THING TO EXPERIENCE, even if we are genuinely "guilty as charged." It is almost unbearable, however, when we are innocent of the wrong for which we are being accused. We bring all of our defenses to bear against such an "attack," and we cannot rest until we are vindicated. The problem, of course, is that we can rarely, if ever, claim such a state of innocence. How many of us can pray honestly with the psalmist: "Judge me, O LORD, according to my righteousness and according to the integrity that is in me" (Ps. 7:8)? How, then, can this psalm be a sincere prayer? How can these words be our own? Perhaps in the following three ways:

First, as has been practiced since the time of the early church, the psalms can be heard as if uttered by the Son of man himself. Only Jesus Christ can lay claim to being utterly sinless in his dealings with others, both friends and enemies alike (4). Prayers for vindication, such as Psalm 7, have been seen by the church as the prayers of the innocent Lamb of God, the only spotless victim before a holy God. When we pray this prayer, we are accompanying our Savior into Jerusalem; before the high priest and Pontius Pilate; betrayed and abandoned by those closest to him; unjustifiably scourged and condemned to the cross; laid low in the dust of death (5).

A second way is to offer these words on behalf of others who are undeservedly suffering violence at the hands of evil. In any region of the world, at any given time, we know that there are new victims of unspeakable cruelty and brutality. And for what fault of theirs? For being in the wrong place at the wrong time; being of the wrong color or language or tribe or religion; being a man or a woman, a child or an old person, who is "in the way"? Are these not all innocent victims who need our prayers for justice and truth to prevail in their otherwise morally inverted worlds?

Finally, as with all of our prayers of lament and complaint, we can make these words our own, even knowing we can claim no pure righteousness, innocence, or worthiness. Accusations, both true and false, will inevitably be made against us. What, then, do we do with the reactions and emotions they trigger? The psalmist teaches us to bring them to the heart of God rather than try to nurse them within our own hearts. "O LORD my God, in *thee* do I take refuge" (1, emphasis added).

FROM THE FATHERS

God alone is the just Judge, he alone is the one who sees hearts. He gives to each one according to his works. Truly, "man looks at the outward appearance" (1 Sam. 16:7), but the Lord is a judge of thoughts and the feelings of the spirit. There is no judgment hidden from him.

Eusebius of Caesarea

I make my complaint to you, O Lord,
   knowing full well that only you know full well
      what is happening to me.
You see how much I thrash about when I feel blamed, or maligned,
   —or just misunderstood.
I will trust you . . . and thank you . . . for being my refuge.
Be the fierce defender and help
   of those who truly suffer injustice.

8

Wednesday of Lent I
PSALM 136

For his steadfast love endures for ever.

v. 1

IT IS TEMPTING AS ONE READS PSALM 136 TO BEGIN skimming over the second half of each verse—the repeated refrain "for his steadfast love endures for ever." At some point, you might ignore it altogether, reading the story being told by the first halves of the verses. But this would miss the point of the hymn altogether. Psalms 135 and 136 are paired in the Jewish liturgy; Psalm 135 tells the same story but without the refrain. Together, the two psalms make up the "Great Hallel" traditionally sung at the conclusion of the Jewish Passover. Quite likely it was the hymn sung by Jesus and the disciples at the Last Supper: "And when they had sung a hymn, they went out to the Mount of Olives" (see Matt. 26:30; Mk. 14:26).

These two psalms review the history of Israel in two different ways. Psalm 135 praises God by presenting a chronological account of his work in creation, and in redeeming the people of Israel. Psalm 136 presents the same story, probably sung by a cantor or choir, but here each statement of what God has done is punctuated with a crisp and joyful declaration of God's love, probably made by the whole congregation. It is as if the poet presents each creative or redemptive act of God as an introductory question which leads to the really important truth to remember. *Why did God do great wonders? Because his mercy endures forever! Why did God bring Israel out of Egypt? Because his mercy endures forever! Why did God lead his people through the wilderness? Because his mercy endures forever! Why does God remember us when we are in trouble? Because his mercy endures forever!*

The Hebrew term *hesed*—sometimes translated as "mercy" or "steadfast love"—has no single English equivalent. Kindness, love, benevolence, *misericordia* in the Latin Vulgate—these have all been used to try to capture the meaning of this singular aspect of God's nature. It belongs to the language of the covenant between God and the Hebrew people. *Hesed* defines the character necessary to honor and fulfill the agreement made between two covenanted parties. In the case of the Psalms (where it appears 127 times!), the word is used again and again to speak of God's faithfulness and loyalty—faithfulness that is rooted in love, and loyalty that is built upon truthfulness. "For his *hesed* endures forever" is both a description of God's eternal commitment to the people in his care, and a charge for those same people to respond to God with faithfulness and love—always.

Psalm 136 stands as a prime example of using repetition to make a point. The cantor throws out each line about a wonderful thing God has done, and the people shout back their refrain of praise. Over and over, divine mercy's rhythm and sound and syllables are repeated. By the time the congregation has finished singing, they may not recall every cry of the cantor, but they will most certainly return home humming their joyful reply.

FROM THE FATHERS

This psalm contains the praise of God, and all its verses finish in the same way. Although many things are related here in praise of God, his mercy is the most commended.

Augustine

It is a good thing for me to give thanks to you, O Lord,
    for your steadfast love to me has come over and over again . . .
        and I can see no end to it, ever.

9

Thursday of Lent I
PSALM 45

My heart overflows with a goodly theme.

v. 1

J ESUS SAID, "THE KINGDOM OF HEAVEN MAY BE COMPARED
to a king who gave a marriage feast for his son" (Matt. 22:2).
This may be the key to appreciating the place of Psalm 45 in
the prayers of the people of God. The poem tells the story of a
royal wedding—the marriage of a Hebrew king (we do not know
which one exactly) to a foreign princess.

The author is clearly a member of the court, perhaps one of
the musicians appointed to sing or play to the praise of God
and for the edification of the king (cf. 1 Kgs. 10:12). The vision
he sees before him, of the king standing before his palace as his
bride and her entourage process to the gates, inspires an overflowing flood of poetic verse. Some he addresses to the king (Ps.
45:2–9)—"I address my verses to the king"—and some to the
bride (10–17)—"Hear, O daughter, consider, and incline your
ear." The beautiful and praiseworthy image is immortalized in
song that, perhaps because it is repeated through generations of

weddings that follow, finds its way to a permanent place within the Psalter and in the prayer of Christ's church.

The Bible presents human marriage as an image of God's covenanted relationship with his people. The prophets spoke in this way (see Isa. 62:5; Jer. 2:2; Hos. 1–3) and so did the apostle Paul (Eph. 5:31–32; 2 Cor. 11:2). It is an image of beauty and grace, of love and gladness, of mutual honor and commitment—in other words, an image of life in the kingdom of God, just as Jesus taught. As one of the church's earliest psalm titles puts it (these were titles assigned to each psalm to assist with their interpretation in the Divine Office): "The fairest in beauty among the sons of men blesses and anoints the Church which the Father has joined to him." The "fairest in beauty" is Jesus Christ himself, and this is certainly how the writer to the Hebrews interpreted the psalm. The angels may reflect the fiery glory of God, but only of the Son can it be said: "God, thy God, has anointed [christened] thee with the oil of gladness beyond thy comrades" (Heb. 1:9).

The marriage being celebrated in Psalm 45 unites the King with the woman of his dreams. Decked in a gold-woven robe ("in splendor . . . holy and without blemish," as Paul describes her—Eph. 5:25–27), his chosen Bride comes to him in humble dignity, and together, "with joy and gladness," they enter the palace. No wonder the visionary John saw heaven as the wedding ceremony *par excellence*: "Let us rejoice and exult and give him the glory, for the marriage of the Lamb has come, and his Bride has made herself ready" (Rev. 19:7).

FROM THE FATHERS

What can be fairer than the soul that is called the daughter of God, and that seeks for itself no outward adorning? She believes in Christ, and dowered with this hope of greatness, makes her way to her spouse, for Christ is at once her bridegroom and her Lord.

Jerome

You see me, Lord, just as I am.
No thing hidden, no thing covered, no thing put-on.
   Yet you still desire me.
You are the fairest—I am the least fair of all.
How can this be?
That such Beauty could see such beauty,
   where beauty has been so lost.
Yet, you see me, Lord, just as I am.

10

Friday of Lent I
PSALM 20

Give victory to the king, O LORD;
answer us when we call.

v. 9

THOUGH OFTEN USED IN THE COMMUNAL LITURGY OF the temple and later the synagogues, most of the psalms were inspired by the personal experiences of their writers. This is readily apparent from the language of the poetry: *I* will give thanks to the Lord; in the Lord *I* will take refuge; hear *my* cry, O God; the Lord delivered *me* in the day of trouble. It is this first-hand, first-person language of the ancient writers that has made the psalms so immediately accessible to every subsequent generation. In Psalm 20, however, "I" appears only one time. In fact, the prayer being offered has nothing to do with the needs of the author—it is all about the needs of another.

Essentially this psalm is a prayer of blessing, probably for the king as he prepares to go out into battle against his enemies. The congregation gathers about him and prays that God will be his help and strength. Look at the rich language of benediction the psalmist uses to express his hope that the king will know God is with him: the Lord *answer* you, *protect* you, *send* you help, *remember* you, *grant* your heart's desire, *fulfill* your hopes, *give* you victory.

Who would not want such a prayer offered on his or her behalf? Whose heart would not be moved to know that others were praying for them in such a way? The intention of the psalmist is that the king would know all the possible ways in which God might uphold his life and assist his endeavors. You do not need to be facing battle for such a prayer to have purpose and meaning. All you need do is consider for a moment those whom you love, who are most important to you, and for whom you wish God's very best. Might this not be a fitting prayer to offer on their behalf?

The prayer is offered from the point of view of one who *knows* that God always comes to the aid of his sons and daughters (Ps. 20:6). To have such confidence for the life of another, the author must have experienced God's saving work in his own life. In the certainty that comes from such trust in "the name of the LORD our God," we can make this our own prayer for family and friends, for public servants and spiritual leaders, and for those who, though unnamed, are not unknown to the Ruler of heaven and earth.

FROM THE FATHERS

When you see others in affliction, comfort them by praying with them in the words of Psalm 20.

Athanasius

This entire psalm voices a prayer as spoken by holy people to the person of Christ. For since for our sakes and on our behalf he received insult when he became man, we are taught to join our prayers with his as he prays and supplicates the Father on our behalf, as one who repels both visible and invisible attacks against us.

Eusibius of Caesarea

I do a lot of praying for myself, Father,
    or at least you hear a lot of hopes and wishes and dreams . . .
        and calls for help.
But, today, I am praying for someone else,
    maybe lots of someone elses:
        people I care for most;
        people I love;
        people who love me;
          and even some people I hardly know at all.
Send them help from your sanctuary, Lord,
And answer all their prayers.

11

Saturday of Lent I
PSALM 139

Whither shall I go from thy Spirit?
Or whither shall I flee from thy presence?

v. 7

SALM 139 IS ONE OF THE MOST PERSONAL AND intimate prayers of the entire Psalter. It is the "I and Thou" of the Hebrew Scriptures. Verse after verse depicts the poet's overwhelming sense that every part of his life is known to God. There is no *place* he can ever be that is beyond God's reach—not the farthest corner of the earth, not the highest reach of heaven, not the deepest void of hell (Ps. 139:6–9). There is no *time* he will ever live that is outside God's omniscient sight—not any day or night, not when he sprang to microscopic life in his mother's womb, not when he lives the very last of his days.

It is tempting to think that verses 19 through 22 ("O that thou wouldst slay the wicked, O God") were not originally part of this psalm. The poet's thought appears more seamless if it is allowed to move directly from verse 18—"when I awake, I am still with thee"—to verse 23—"search me, O God, and know my heart." But there is no indication in the Hebrew that the

intervening verses are taken from any other source. The psalmist's invective against the wicked seems to be his way of taking
God's side against those who stand against God: "Do I not hate
them that hate thee, O LORD? . . . I count them *my* enemies"
(21–22, emphasis added). In other words: *You, Lord, are always
and everywhere profoundly concerned for me. I want you to know that I am
also concerned for you.* In the sometimes coarse and always honest
language of prayer and poetry, the psalmist speaks what is in
his heart with brutal directness.

Still, the author knows that all the varied movements of that
heart—for good and for evil—are known to God and to God
alone. He begins by saying God has already searched and known
him (1). He spends most of the psalm trying to describe the
unfathomable mystery of God's omniscience—not in general
categories, but in verses of personal testimony. Now, at the end,
he says, *Try me and prove me. My heart is an open book to you. Tell me
how its lines read to you. Let me know what uneven rhythms its verses contain.
And, above all else, continue to lead me in your ways, the ways that are
everlasting* (23–24).

FROM THE FATHERS

Do you see how prudent the [psalmist] is and how grateful is his
heart? What he is saying is this: "I thank you that I have a Master
whom I cannot comprehend." . . . What he is speaking of here is
God's omnipresence; and he is showing that this is the very thing
that he does not understand, namely, how God is present everywhere—"If I go up to heaven you are there; if I go down to hell,
you are present." Do you see how God is everywhere present?

[The psalmist] did not know how this is true, but he shudders, he is upset, he is at a loss when he so much as thinks about it.

John Chrysostom

My understanding is no better than the psalmist's, Lord.
I cannot begin to fathom the breadth of your vision;
 nor the reach of your arms; nor the spread of your wings.
I would, however, have my mind as full of wonder,
  and my mouth as full of praise,
   as what I read in these lines.
And my heart as full of humility.

12

Second Sunday of Lent
PSALM 145

Great is the LORD, and greatly to be praised,
and his greatness is unsearchable.

v. 3

*P*RAISE—THIS SINGLE WORD IN THE SUPERSCRIPTION*
of Psalm 145 summarizes the twenty-one verses that
follow. The psalmist has made an acrostic with the words,
beginning each verse with a successive letter of the Hebrew
alphabet. If the content itself is not enough, the familiar poetic
technique makes the point clear: *everyone* and *everything*—from *aleph*
to *tav*, from A to Z—is called upon to praise the Lord!

Psalm 145 introduces the final psalms—the so-called "Praise
Psalms"—of the collection we know as the Psalter. How entirely
fitting. These last five prayers all begin with the same word, the
same jubilant imperative: *Hallelujah!* Praise the Lord! Notice how
Psalm 145 provides a transition from prayers of petition that pre-
cede it to the prayers of praise that follow. From here to the end of
the Psalter, you will not find a single request being made of God.

---

*   The superscription, found at the start of many psalms, is a prefatory
    verse that explains the setting or authorship of the psalm or gives musical
    instruction.

The only "request" is made of God's handiwork, God's creatures, God's people—that together they bless God's name forever.

In this brief prayer, God's name appears fourteen times, and the Hebrew word for "all" or "every" is repeated nineteen times. In the joy of overflowing praise, the psalmist calls upon voices of all places and every generation to declare God's mighty acts and to proclaim his glory. From the single voice of the first verse—"*I* will extol thee, my God" (emphasis added)—to the universal cry of the final verse—"let *all* flesh bless his holy name" (emphasis added)— the psalmist builds his prayer to a crescendo of exaltation.

What inspires such ecstatic expression? The psalmist is unable to find words sufficient to describe what he knows to be true about God. He looks to his own experience and that of others (of the whole world, in fact) and offers one word after another to attempt to express what he introduces in verse 3 as the unsearchable *greatness* of God: gracious, merciful, slow to anger, abounding in steadfast love, good to all, compassionate, powerful, holy, faithful, just, kind, near. And look at all the verbs used to describe God's actions: upholds, raises up, gives, opens, satisfies, fulfills, hears, preserves, saves. Hardly any other psalm can compete with the intensity of emotion and the efficiency of language within these short verses. "Can any praise be worthy of the Lord's majesty?" asks St. Augustine in his *Confessions*. Perhaps not. But Psalm 145 certainly comes close.

FROM THE FATHERS

The fact that the divine greatness has no limit is proclaimed by the prophecy, which declares expressly that of God's splendor, his glory and his holiness, "there is no end." . . . For by what name can I describe the incomprehensible? By what speech can I declare the unspeakable? Since God is too excellent and lofty to be expressed in words, we have learned to honor in silence what transcends speech and thought.

Gregory of Nyssa

Perhaps praiseful silence
    is the best response I can offer to your glory, Lord.
Holy awe usually does not speak. It only listens.
But if from time to time I do not give my heart a voice,
    then I do not give you your due,
        and I do not give my own breath its reason to breathe.
So I will extol you, my God, and bless your name forever and ever.

13

Monday of Lent II
PSALM 41

Blessed is he who considers the poor.

v. 1

THE VERSE OF ISAIAH WE MIGHT READ TRANSLATED from the Hebrew as, "Surely he has borne our griefs and carried our sorrows" (Isa. 53:4) could also say, "Surely he has borne our *sicknesses* and carried our *pains*." The language of the poetry conveys the intimate connection that exists between physical, emotional, and spiritual suffering. We are "spirit and soul and body" (1 Thess. 5:23) and the inflictions we suffer make their harmful impact on our whole person. Psalm 41 is the prayer of one who knows this firsthand.

The psalmist has fallen deathly ill, too weak to lift his body or his spirit by himself. On the one hand, he counts on God's promise to sustain and bless those who are mindful of others who are weak or infirmed (Ps. 41:1–3). He counts himself among those whom God will heal because of the compassion he has shown to those in the same condition in which he now finds himself. "Be gracious to me, and raise me up" (10) is a prayer of trust in the midst of his pain. On the other hand, the psalmist's malady is not physical alone, and for this—the worst part of his suffering—he cries out with complaining and grief (4–9).

He readily acknowledges his unrighteous and unworthy condition before God—"I have sinned against thee" (4), and it might be bearable if personal sin and grave illness alone were his adversaries. But those who oppose him see in his weakened condition the opportunity to conspire—literally, to "whisper together" (7)—against him. In the scene set by the psalmist, one can almost hear their malicious hisses as, just outside the door, they plot his demise. But far more demoralizing is the betrayal of one of his dearest ("bosom") friends (9). This is the worst pain of all. In the Hebrew culture of the time, where oath-taking and meal-sharing are virtually synonymous, and where fidelity is celebrated as the supreme virtue, betrayal by a companion who has eaten at one's own table is tantamount to an unforgiveable sin.

One cannot read these words without hearing them on the lips of Jesus at the Last Supper (John 13:18), and so this psalm has taken its place among many that are heard as a prayer of our Savior. Perhaps that is the best key to understanding its message.

FROM THE FATHERS

God will heal you if only you admit your wound. You lie under the physician's hands; patiently implore his aid. If he bathes or burns or cuts it, bear it calmly; do not even pay any attention to it, provided you are cured. Moreover, you will be cured if you present yourself to the doctor. Not that he does not see you hide, but confession is the beginning of restoration to health.

Caesarius of Arles

I can never fully measure, Lord, the depth of betrayal you suffered
      at the hand of your friend.
But I needn't point to Judas to find your only traitor.
      Is it I, Lord?
            I know it is.
But just as deep—deeper still—is your compassion.
For it is you, Lord, who consider the poor.

14

Tuesday of Lent II
PSALM 35

Say to my soul, "I am your deliverance!"

v. 3

SINCE THE EARLIEST USE OF THE PSALTER IN CHRISTIAN prayer, the church has heard at least two "voices" in the psalms—the voice of Christ's people, and the voice of Christ himself. In other words, the psalms may be prayers *to* Christ or *by* Christ. In Psalm 35, we can hear these two voices loud and clear.

As a prayer *by* Christ, Psalm 35 accurately and poignantly describes the hours of his passion—his betrayal, arrest, trial, and condemnation to death. Consider the images used to depict his enemies: fighters, pursuers, hunters, traitors, schemers, lying witnesses, mockers, wild animals, haters. The Gospel accounts of Jesus's final hours are filled with people who fit these fiendish labels. In his final teaching to his followers (John 14–17), Jesus speaks of many things, including the suffering he is about to endure. Only once does he quote from Hebrew Scriptures, turning to Psalm 35 as the best description for what he is facing: "It is to fulfill the word that is written in their law, 'They hated me without a cause'" (John 15:25, quoting Ps. 35:19; see also Ps. 69:4). When we hear the voice of Christ in this psalm, we come alongside him in his suffering, and understand better what the writer to the Hebrews meant when he said: "In the days of his flesh, Jesus offered up prayers and supplications, with loud cries and tears, to him who was able to save him from death, *and he was heard* for his godly fear" (Heb. 5:7, emphasis added).

As a prayer *to* Christ, Psalm 35 gathers our own experiences of fear and pain, and brings them honestly before God. This is where the psalms do us the colossal favor of giving us truthful language with which to "curse" our enemies—our *enemies* being impossible circumstances, the anguish of our own sin, those who actually hate us, or the "spiritual forces of wickedness" that do battle against us—so that we, like Jesus, can be *heard* by our Father in heaven.

In the fourth century, a perilous time of persecution against the church, Bishop Athanasius told his congregation, "If enemies persist, and, with hands red with blood, try to drag you down and kill you, remember that God is the proper judge, and so say the words of Psalm 35." Ultimately—and especially when looking to the example of Jesus—these words remind us that God is our salvation (Ps. 35:3), that he delights in our well-being (27), and that praise for his deliverance will always have the last word (10, 18, 28).

FROM THE FATHERS

I will seek no salvation other than the Lord my God. . . . Even in your temporal problems it is God who helps you through human agency, for he is your salvation. . . . All things are subject to him, and he undoubtedly supports our temporal life, differently in the case of each person. . . . Let us all call on him, brothers and sisters

. . . to open our spiritual ears so that we may hear him saying, "I am your salvation." He says it, but some of us are getting deaf, so that when we find ourselves in trouble, we prefer to listen to the enemies that harry us.

Augustine

Lord Jesus, you honor me
when you let me use your prayers.
But already you have honored me
when you let me live your life.
Blessings, troubles, peace, suffering, joy, sorrow
—death and resurrection—
My life is hid with Christ.
May my prayers be also.

15

Wednesday of Lent II
PSALM 37

For the wicked shall be cut off;
but those who wait for the LORD shall possess the land.

v. 9

PSALM 37 IS ANOTHER ACROSTIC PSALM (ONE OF twelve in all), though in this case it is essentially each set of two verses that begins with successive letters of the Hebrew alphabet. Even more interesting, perhaps, is that God is never addressed in this psalm. There are words *about* God, but never *to* God. It reads more like a chapter from Proverbs than a song of praise or lament to the Lord (e.g., see Prov. 2:21–22; 16:3; 20:24; 23:17; 24:1). Usually when we think of prayer, we think of speaking to God—praising, thanking, interceding, asking, seeking, and knocking. Psalm 37 reminds us of an equally vital aspect of prayer (perhaps the most vital?)—*listening*.

Writing to Christians undergoing persecution in Asia Minor, the apostle Peter devoted an entire letter to urging patience in their suffering—to refrain from vengeful thoughts or actions, to believe in the just ways of God, and to hope in the promised future (see 1 Pet. 1:6–7, 13; 2:1; 3:9; 4:1–2, 12–13). When he gave these admonitions to the next generation of Christian disciples, Peter was an old man, nearing the end of his own race and speaking from the vantage point of age and years of experience. One hears the same wise tone in Psalm 37. The author of Psalm 37 brings all of his skills of persuasion to bear—encouragement, admonition, warning, promise, and illustration—for the sake of teaching his younger disciple not to abandon his or her faith in God, but to hold fast and "trust in the Lord."

Woven through the poet's message is an allegory familiar to the Hebrew mind: "Wait for the LORD, and *keep to his way*, and he will exalt you *to possess the land*" (Ps. 37:34, emphasis added). All of life is like the journey of our forebears to the Promised Land. Five times the psalmist reminds his listener that the faithful will "possess the land" and five times he declares that the wicked will be "cut off." To the "youthful" listener who looks for immediate results of justice and reward (in this way, most all of us are "youthful"), the journey includes many injustices and disappointments. In fact, the wicked often *do* prosper, and good people, including the pilgrim, suffer. In the face of all this, do not give up, exhorts the wise psalmist. I have lived long enough to see the wicked and their deeds blow away like the dust, and to see the faithful come into their final reward. *Listen* to what I am saying.

FROM THE FATHERS

What seems slow to you is swift to God; submit yourself to God, and it will seem swift to you as well. . . . This present time is your winter. Your glory does not show yet. . . . You look as dead as the trees do in winter, parched and apparently lifeless. What hope have we, then, if we are dead? We have the root [of charity] within us, and where our root is fixed, there is our life, for there is our charity. How can anyone with such a root ever wilt? But when will spring arrive for us? Or our summer? When shall we be arrayed in fair foliage or laden with luscious fruit? When shall that be? "When Christ appears, Christ who is your life, then you too will appear with him in glory" (Col. 3:3–4).

Augustine

Father, "My life is hid with Christ."
So hid, though, that sometimes I cannot see it myself,
especially when it is covered with ice and snow.
Still, my life is hid with Christ . . . so when he appears . . .
What will he find?

16

Thursday of Lent II
PSALM 50

"Gather to me my faithful ones,
who made a covenant with me by sacrifice!"

v. 5

W HAT WE HAVE HERE IS A COSMIC ARRAIGNMENT, with all of the legal vocabulary and activity of a judicial hearing. Unlike any earthly trial, however, the Judge is also the witness for the prosecution, and the prosecutor . . . *and* the plaintiff. And why shouldn't he be? He is the Mighty One, Yahweh, the Origin and Creator of the universe, whose sovereign rule extends from horizon to horizon and through all times and seasons. Heaven and earth testify to his supreme authority. When he calls and summons a gathering, no quarter is given for refusal or defiance. Announced by raging fire and accompanied by tempestuous winds, God takes his seat before the assembly, and everything, everyone, falls silent. Not a word is uttered. Not a sound is made as he brings his indictment, making his irrefutable case against the defendant.

And who is it that stands alone and powerless before Yahweh? "Hear, O *my* people," God addresses them. "I am God, *your* God" (Ps. 50:7, emphasis added). The defendant is God's own people, with whom he has made a covenant; they have promised to follow him to the end of their days. The defendant is us. The defendant is me. In language reminiscent of the great *Shema* of Mount Sinai—"Hear, O Israel" (Deut. 6:4)—God now commands those whom he claimed for his own on that mountain, and who in turn claimed him for their own, to stand silently and listen to his judgments against them:

> I have no argument with your rituals or the practices of your worship. You make your sacrifices according to the law, and I see them every day. But they are empty of meaning because they are empty of gratitude. They are empty of devotion. They are empty of love. Day after day you read and recite my words, but you do not let them penetrate your hearts. You offer your sacrifice to me, but then you go out and steal from your neighbor. The hurtful words you speak in secret are louder than the pious prayers you bring to my altar. And all the time you think I do not know what is going on in your heart. How can you call upon *my* name when *yours* is the only name you really care about?*

---

* It would be naive of us to think that such an indictment would be reserved only for the psalmist's immediate listeners. Saint Paul brought much the same message to the Christians in Corinth who regularly gathered to celebrate the Lord's Supper, but who cared not a whit for one another (see 1 Cor. 11:17–34). Hypocrisy is an especially insidious sin for religious people. "Not every one who says to me, 'Lord, lord,' shall enter the kingdom of heaven" (Matt. 7:21).

We don't know how those in the dock answered to the charges made against them. The only one who speaks in Psalm 50 is God. But whoever arranged the order of the Psalter surely saw in the psalm that follows, Psalm 51, the only appropriate response: "Have mercy on me, O God . . . for I know my transgressions. . . . Create in me a clean heart, O God, and put a new and right spirit within me" (Ps. 51:1, 3, 10).

FROM THE FATHERS

"Offer to God a sacrifice of praise." Praise, in fact, is nothing other than commendation, glory, and blessing. So, let your life be of such a kind as to bless your Master, and you have performed the perfect sacrifice.

John Chrysostom

I stand guilty as charged, Lord.
So I kneel to make my answer:
Lord, have mercy on me.

17

Friday of Lent II
PSALM 54

Save me, O God, by thy name.

v. 1

A BENEDICTINE SISTER AND LONG-TIME STUDENT of the psalms tells the story of her early years in the monastery when she taught a course on the Psalter to a group of older sisters. When the class came to the "cursing" psalms (such as Psalm 54), one venerable sister exclaimed, "I can't say those things in church!" Our young teacher, assuming that her elder's many years of experience had mellowed her to a state of holy patience and forgiveness, was about to say that she didn't have to, when suddenly one of her contemporaries blurted out, "I don't know why you can't say them in church. You say them in the hall!"[3] One key for understanding and praying the cursing psalms is to know ourselves well enough to understand that we are one and the same person in church and in the hall.

The superscription of Psalm 54 attributes the prayer to David while he was in hiding from Saul, as recounted in 1 Samuel 23. The Ziphites, in whose hill country David had found refuge, went to Saul and gave up the location of their famous refuge. "Now come down, O king," they schemed, "according to all your heart's desire to come down; and our part shall be to surrender him into the king's hand" (1 Sam. 23:20). One can imagine David, or any other person who has entrusted him or herself to the protection of another, hearing of the betrayal and crying out to God in fear and in rage against such traitors.

But with all the common characteristics of a lament, this psalm also carries something of a confident tone, the tone of someone who has had such an experience before, and knows already that he will be heard and delivered. "God is my helper; the Lord is the upholder of my life" (Ps. 54:4). Even as he prays for protection and vindication, even as he wishes to "put an end to" (5) his enemies, the psalmist entrusts his well-being to the One who has proven his power and love already.

Psalms such as these can be of great help to us in expressing the darker thoughts and dispositions of our hearts. Beyond this, they help us to move *through* them to genuine trust, and even to praise. The name in which the psalmist longs for his salvation—"Save me, O God, by thy name" (1)—is the same name to which he will dedicate his praise in the temple—"I will give thanks to thy name, O LORD" (6). It is a name—the *only* name—that can be relied upon, for it, too, has plumbed the depths of human despair, and risen to the heights of divine glory. It is the name which is above every name and to which all other names shall inevitably bend the knee.

FROM THE FATHERS

The suffering of the prophet David is . . . a type of the passion of our God and Lord Jesus Christ. This is why David's prayer also corresponds in sense with the prayer of Christ, who being the Word, was made flesh. . . . He, who bore human infirmities and took on himself the sins of people, approached God in prayer with the humility proper to human beings. . . . For he says, "Save me, O God, by your name." Thus [Christ] prays in bodily humiliation, using the words of his own prophet.

Hilary of Poitiers

Lord, my lament is rarely if ever because of a threat to my life,
but usually because of a threat to my life as I would like it to be.
Still, I do need to be saved from my enemies,
from all those forces—within and without—
that would sell me out for a pittance.

18

Saturday of Lent II
PSALM 62

For God alone my soul waits in silence.

v. 1

THE SAYING GOES THAT A MAN WHO IS HIS OWN lawyer has a fool for a client. The same could probably be said about self-reliance of any kind: self-diagnosis, self-counsel, self-direction, self-defense. Giving advice to oneself is always risky business, but if that advice includes saying to one's soul in times of trouble, "Look to God for help," then, as Psalm 62 demonstrates, talking to oneself might not be so foolish after all.

"For God alone my soul waits in silence." The psalm begins with a moment of eavesdropping. It is almost as if we are let in on the quiet thoughts of the psalmist as he sits alone on a rock wall outside the temple. It is not exactly a prayer we are hearing. More like a musing. The psalmist is talking to himself: *Listen, my soul. Wait for God to come. You know who he is: your help and strength; stronger than the rock you are sitting on and certainly more impenetrable than the temple you see before you. Once he comes along side, nothing can knock you over.*

The psalmist's address moves from his own soul to his adversaries. Once he has reminded himself of God's matchless power, he has the confidence to speak directly to those people / circumstances / inner convulsions of heart which would throw him to the ground: *How long do you plan to keep this up? Do you really think that you can do me in with your empty threats? I may be nothing more than a weak and wobbly wall, but you are up against more than me. My real home is in a Rock. I live in a Fortress that you cannot even shake, much less raze. He is my refuge* (see Ps. 62:6).

Now the psalmist is on a roll. We can see him straighten himself and turn ever so slightly to face another audience. He has dispatched his enemies. This time it is his friends he addresses. It is the people with whom he prays in the temple everyday: *You live in this Fortress, too. Trust in him, always. Pour out every anxious thought in your heart. Let him know everything about you. You see those people / circumstances / inner convulsions of heart all around you. There's nothing to them. They are lighter than air. Whatever you do, don't look to them for help, ever* (see 9–10).

The psalmist seems now to turn inward again. His eyes close and his head bows. His final words are addressed to God alone. What began with giving himself "a good talking to" ends with prayer: *You, Lord, are all the power and love that I need. You are my Lord.* Psalm 62 is self-direction at its very best, for it points to Another, as it should. *Listen, my soul. Talk to God.*

FROM THE FATHERS

Hope in [God]; do not trust in your own powers. Confess your bad things to him; hope for your good things from him. Without his help you will be nothing, however proud you may be. So, in order that you may be enabled to be humble, "pour out your hearts before him"; and to avoid remaining wrongly stuck on yourselves, say what comes next: "God is our helper."

Augustine

My soul, if you have anything to say today, do not say it to me.
I cannot be of much help to you.
But I know who can be.
Tell him everything.

19

Third Sunday of Lent

PSALM 27

"Thy face, LORD, do I seek."

v. 8

IF EVER THERE WAS A SONG OF SUPREME TRUST AND confidence in God, it is Psalm 27. Its opening line—"The LORD is my light and my salvation; whom shall I fear?" (Ps. 27:1)—strikes the same chord as that of Psalm 23: "The LORD is my shepherd, I shall not want" (Ps 23:1). The messages are alike: *There is nothing beside my Lord that I need; there is nothing beside my Lord that I fear. In each case, the psalmist's confidence is unshakable.*

The source of his confidence is the Lord alone. No one else. Both the first and final word of Psalm 27 is *Yahweh*, the Lord. Beginning and End. And sandwiched between those two, the divine name appears eleven more times in twelve brief verses. Few psalms have such a concentration of this one-word confession of faith. Probably the best New Testament counterpart would be the eighth chapter of Paul's Letter to the Romans: "I am sure that neither death nor life . . . nor anything else in all creation, will be able to separate us from the love of God in Christ Jesus our Lord" (Rom. 8:38–39). *Yahweh–Yeshua.* Jesus Christ—the light of the world and the salvation of my soul—is the same yesterday, today, and forever.

Perhaps, in part, it is for this reason that Psalm 27 finds itself among the psalms traditionally sung at Matins on Good Friday, under the title, "False witnesses rise against me and iniquity has lied to itself." Not only because the psalm expresses such trust in God's defending power, but because in the shadow of Good Friday darkness (which can overshadow *any* day of the year), the psalmist looks to a promised, radiant future: "I believe that I shall see the goodness of the LORD in the land of the living" (Ps. 27:13). Light out of darkness; trust out of fear; life out of death. Commenting on the similar Psalm 121, Augustine wrote: "Guard yourselves, but not by any strength of your own, for the Lord is your defense and your guardian, the Lord who neither grows drowsy nor sleeps. Once only did he sleep for us, but he rose again, and now he will never sleep anymore."[4]

Lest we think that the author of Psalm 27 was infused with this confident trust from birth, we must read the words of the whole psalm. His heart takes courage, and he exhorts his listeners' hearts to do the same (14), because he knows the bitter taste of abandonment (10), the pain of betrayal (12); and the suffering of evil (2). But in and through it all, he has remained determined to "face forward" to the face of God. There is one thing he asks of God, and one thing he expects of himself (4): to seek the presence of God all the days of his life. Psalm 27 tells us that confidence *in* God comes from being *with* God.

FROM THE FATHERS

"Whom shall I fear?" means "I shall fear no one." Fear of the Lord
had ensured that he could fear no other.

Cassiodorus

Such confidence as this seems beyond my reach, Lord.
But this can only mean that I am reaching for the wrong thing.
In the midst of the shadows that overtake me
It is not confidence for which I must reach
    (for confidence has no face to attract me)
I must reach for you . . .
    and confidence will come with the sparkle in your eye.

20

Monday of Lent III
PSALM 71

My mouth is filled with thy praise.

v. 8

IN THE ACCOUNT OF THE MARTYRDOM OF POLYCARP, a disciple of John the Apostle and bishop of Smyrna in Asia Minor (see Rev. 2:8–11), he is arrested during a time of persecution and threatened with death unless he should renounce his faith in Christ. He responds to the Roman proconsul: "Eighty-six years have I served him and he has done me no wrong. How can I blaspheme the King who saved me?"* If anyone would understand and appreciate the words of Psalm 71, it would be Polycarp, for this psalm is the prayer and testimony of one who is gray-haired and "full of years," and determined to praise his God to his very last breath.

The message of Psalm 71 cannot be taught; it can only be lived. The psalmist is in his twilight years and from that vantage point he looks at his present circumstances, his past experiences, and his future expectations—and he sees God *everywhere*. His petition to be saved once again is founded upon the scores of troubles he has encountered and from which God has "revived" him (Ps.

---

* Assuming the count of his years serving Christ starts with his conversion rather than birth, Polycarp was likely even older.

71:20). His faith now burns not with the fury of youthful, crack-
ling flames, but with the constancy and intensity of glowing coals.
When he looks at his present condition—old age (18); strength
is spent (9); adversaries are relentless (10–11); head bowed down
and soul driven to the ground (20)—he looks only through the
lens of his lifelong relationship with God and of God's lifelong
fidelity to him: My God, you have been with me from day one. In
fact, you were my mother's midwife; when I came from the womb,
I fell into your arms (6). You raised me and taught me (17) and led
me to and through many, many miseries (20). His entire life has
been written in the narrative of an unbreakable companionship.

So now, as he faces his inability to take on the forces that come
against him, what does he do? "My praise is continually of thee"
(6); "My mouth is filled with thy praise" (v. 8); "I . . . will praise thee
yet more and more" (14); "My lips will shout for joy" (23). And:
"My mouth will tell of thy righteous acts" (15); "I still proclaim thy
wondrous deeds" (17); "I proclaim thy might to all the generations
to come" (18); "My tongue will talk of thy righteous help all the
day long" (24). What he has always done he will continue to do.
Praise and worship, proclaim and testify, rejoice and give thanks—
how could he stop now? How could he ever blaspheme the King
who saved him?

FROM THE FATHERS

A great contest earns great glory; not human or temporal glory,
but divine and eternal. Faith is doing battle; and when faith is
doing battle, nobody can overthrow the flesh. Because even if it
is mangled and torn to shreds, when can anyone perish who has

been redeemed by the blood of Christ? A powerful person will not lose what he has bought with his gold; how can Christ lose what he has bought with his blood?

Augustine

> *Habits are born of repeated practice, Lord.*
> *I know this, because I have many bad ones, well-practiced.*
> *But if there is a habit that I would like to have,*
> > *and never to break,*
> > *it is the habit of praise.*
> *There is only one way, you say.*
> *Practice, practice, practice.*

21

Tuesday of Lent III
PSALM 77

I will remember thy wonders of old.

v. 11

WHEN YOU CANNOT SLEEP, WHATEVER THE CAUSE, the middle of the night can be like a windowless, wall-less void. The creeping passage of time stops being measured and can only be endured. Worst of all, the darkness of the bedroom becomes matched only by the darkness of your mind, which seems incapable of refusing any anxious or troublesome thought that knocks at its door. Worries that you thought were put to rest suddenly arise like wild animals. Unresolved arguments get replayed over and over again and hurt feelings are nursed into full-grown resentments. But mostly it is the fears that take hold. Fears for ourselves and our circumstances; fears for our loved ones and their circumstances; fears of things unknown and unwanted; fears that the dawn is too far off to reach in one emotional piece. Anyone who has experienced such a night—and, sooner or later, we all do—may find the words of Psalm 77 both familiar and helpful.

It sounds like the psalmist has experienced a number of nights like this. Probably many (see Ps. 77:2, 4, 6). The particular problem is never made explicit, making Psalm 77 "flexible" enough for any of us to use, but there is a Job-like quality to the poet's suffering. I cry out, I seek, I stretch for and I think about *you*, O God, but you are not there (1–6). In his despair at not finding God, the psalmist begins to doubt, and then to question. Are you ignoring me? Have you forgotten me and the promises you once made to me? Worse yet, are you now angry with me? So angry that you will have no mercy? (7–9). Finding no help and hearing no answer, our sleepless poet shakes his fist at the dark and makes his final accusation: God has changed. He either *cannot* help me (his "right hand" of power is too weak), or *will* not help me (his "right hand" of love is withheld) (10).

A long, dark night can be like a magnifying glass that turns even the smallest crevices in our faith into vast canyons of unbelief. When that happens, the rest of Psalm 71 may offer us a gentle guide out of the darkness. "I will call to mind the deeds of the LORD; yea, I will remember thy wonders of old" (11). Verse 11 is the turning point in the psalm, moving from questioning to declaring, from doubting to believing. In the final ten verses, there is no sign of a specific answer to the anguish expressed in the first ten verses. We are not given to know if God ever came to the psalmist's rescue. What we do hear, however, is the psalmist reaching *back*, far before his own lifetime, to the most pivotal event (to that point) in the history of God's saving deeds—the parting of the Red Sea, a passing over of God's people from death to life. No wonder Psalm 77 has come to be sung on the evening of Holy

Thursday. Facing the longest night of the year, it recalls what God has already done and hints at the rising sun to come.

FROM THE FATHERS

"My hands were stretched out by night.". . . Searching by night occurs in this world when the truth has not yet shed light. This world will certainly come to an end and will meet Christ [in judgment]. And when Christ comes, he will be like the sun shining in the hearts of all people.

Caesarius of Arles

> *When my spirit is so troubled that it cannot rest;*
> *When my heart is so pressed that it cannot breathe;*
> *When my mind is so dark that it cannot see;*
> *I will remember that you rolled the stone away.*

22

Wednesday of Lent III
PSALM 109

He loved to curse; let curses come on him!

v. 17

HERE ARE MORE PSALMS OF LAMENTATION IN THE
Psalter than any other kind—more than praises, more
than petitions, more than thanksgivings, more than
intercessions. No doubt this says a great deal about the human
condition and about the nature of prayer. Weakness, need,
anguish: these must all be expressed honestly before God, even
to the point of crying and groaning, if praise and thanksgiving
are to be authentic (see Rom. 8:26, 31). Among the psalms of
lament are the so-called "cursing psalms," prayers in which the
psalmist denounces his or her enemies and pleads with God to
punish them, such as Psalm 54 mentioned earlier. These psalms
present human emotion in some of its rawest forms. And, among
these cursing psalms, there is none more acrid and indignant
than Psalm 109. The bitterness of the psalmist pours out like
liquid fire upon the wicked. Nothing less than divine retribution
will satisfy. At the heart of it, the prayer asks that the one who
curses will himself be cursed—his life shortened; his family

left desolate; his possessions plundered; his name vilified; his memory obliterated. "He clothed himself with cursing . . . may it soak into his body . . . like oil into his bones" (Ps. 109:18).

As disciples of a Master who instructed us to love our enemies, to pray for those who hate us, and to turn the other cheek when we are unjustly struck, what are we to make of the kind of language we encounter in this psalm? More importantly, if it is a prayer, how can we possibly make it our own prayer? Such questions have been discussed (which is a nonpsalm-like word for "fought over"!) for as long as the Psalter has been used in the church. We cannot hope to settle the issue in a couple of paragraphs. But as we read this psalm—and perhaps even pray it—we can keep this in mind: the vocabulary of cursing is not limited to the Old Testament.* The words of mercy we hear from the lips of Jesus should never be mistaken for indifference to evil. We cannot be so selective about Jesus's teaching or his actions. Remember his judgment against the "goats" gathered on his left hand (Matt. 25:41–46); his invectives against the scribes and Pharisees (Matt. 23:13–36); his indictment of unrepentant cities (Lk. 10:13); his "cleansing" of the temple (John 2:14–15)? Perhaps his harshest censure was reserved for those who injured the innocent, for whom (in language reminiscent of Psalm 109) drowning in the sea would be a just penalty (Matt. 18:6–7). The message of Jesus *fulfills* the message of the Old Testament; it does not repudiate it. *Both* blessing and damnation are fundamental, albeit mysterious, components in the economy of God.

---

* In the Old Testament, at times, it appears in an almost ritualized form (e.g., Deut. 27:15–26; 28:15–46).

When the earliest members of the church sought to replace Judas, they turned to Psalm 109 to explain their actions.* One way we can make Psalm 109 our own prayer is when we curse the *real* enemies of the human soul: faithlessness, betrayal, hatred, despair, injustice, cruelty. Another is to remember that such evils inhabit, and destroy, real flesh and blood—the same flesh and blood as Judas's, the same flesh and blood as yours and mine.

FROM THE FATHERS
Made heirs of your blessing, Lord, we may not fear the curses of your enemies. Although they have spoken evil against my soul, you, Lord, O Lord, help me according to your great mercy.

Fifth-century psalm collect for Psalm 109

If you hear my prayers, O Lord,
You hear all *of my prayers,*
     —even those I barely say . . . but clearly feel.

---

*   Acts 1:20 quotes from the Septuagint translation of Ps. 109:8.

23

Thursday of Lent III
PSALM 105

Remember the wonderful works that he has done.

v. 5

PSALMS 104 THROUGH 107 FOCUS UPON THE HISTORY of God's people, more precisely upon the history of God's actions on behalf of his people.* Each does so in its own particular way, but a common message in their verses is that, even amid all of the uncertainties presented by human fickleness, failure, and fault, God will have his way. Taken together or standing alone, these prayers present a convincing argument for the declaration made by St. Paul in Romans 8:28: "We know that in everything God works for good with those who love him, who are called according to his purpose."

In the case of Psalm 105, the call to "give thanks to the LORD," to sing to him and to praise him (Ps. 105:1–3) is based upon that most fundamental of all requirements for living faithfully in the kingdom of God: "*Remember* the wonderful works that he has done" (5, emphasis added). While Psalm 104 recites those "wonderful

---

* See also Psalms 78 and 136.

works" as they were made known in creation, Psalm 105 concen-
trates on God's providential handiwork for the people whom he
subsequently "anointed" to be his own (15). To do so, the psalmist
summarizes three stories: the covenant with the patriarchs—
Abraham, Isaac, and Jacob (12–15); the appointment and preparation of Joseph (16–22); and the exodus of Israel from Egypt,
including God's miraculous provision for them in the wilderness
(23–41). These are among the events that made a mighty nation
out of an unknown handful of desert nomads, and the psalmist
does not want anyone to forget them.

Furthermore, it is not only for the name of Israel that God
has performed these mighty deeds. It is also for the sake of his
own name—his own reputation, if you will. The psalmist's call
to God's people—to *us*—to remember is based upon God also
remembering. God intervenes and works because "he is mindful
of his covenant . . . of the word that he commanded" to Abraham
and his posterity (8–9). He provided a way in the desert, and
will continue to provide a way, because "he remembered his holy
promise" (42). Everything that God has done and will do is rooted
in his faithfulness. He made a promise, and he is a God of his
word. The good that comes out of his purposes is inevitable.

The first fifteen verses of Psalm 105 comprise one of the three
songs sung by Asaph and his Levite brethren on the day that David
brings the ark of the covenant into Jerusalem (1 Chr. 16:7–22).
The record tells us that the king "appointed that thanksgiving be
sung to the LORD" in the presence of the most sacred and cherished
sign of God's promise to his people. Now that the temple is
destroyed, and a new Temple has risen in its place (John 2:19–20),
can anything less be expected of us?

FROM THE FATHERS

I implore you, dearly beloved, always to call to mind and remember what has been said for the salvation of your soul. Do not accept it only in passing. [God's] word ought to fasten its roots in your heart, so that on judgment day it may happily bear the fruits of eternal life.

Caearius of Arles

Forgetfulness is no excuse for my sin, Father,
But it is often a cause of it.
Forgetting your love . . . my need . . . your Son . . . my blessings.
Remembering is no guarantee against my sin, Father,
But it is often be a remedy for it.

24

Friday of Lent III

PSALM 119

Oh, how I love thy law!

v. 97

W E BEGIN BY STATING THE OBVIOUS: AT 176 verses, Psalm 119 is the longest of the psalms. But the psalm's length is not arbitrary and has a great deal to do with its meaning. Its structure enhances that meaning even further. Psalm 119 is another of the acrostic psalms,* though with a twist. There are twenty-two sections—one for each letter of the Hebrew alphabet—and eight lines in each section—each beginning with that same Hebrew letter. Quite a feat of poetic construction. Just try writing eight lines of poetry, each beginning with the letter X!

Neither the psalm's length nor its structure is meant to impress, however. Rather, they are meant to emphasize. There are three primary participants in the psalm: the psalmist, God, and Torah. The first three verses are introductory, written in the third person, and sound a familiar theme—blessing comes from walking in the way of the Lord. From that point on, the psalmist addresses God directly and, for 173 verses, returns again and again to a single

---

* The others are Pss. 9, 10, 25, 34, 37, 111,112, 145.

idea: the keeping of *torah*, the "law" of God. The word *torah* is used twenty-five times, and together with all of its various synonyms—law, precepts, statutes, testimonies, ordinances, judgments, commandments, decrees, promise, path, way—it appears in almost every verse of the psalm. With the rhythm and repetition of chanted incantation, Psalm 119 finds dozens of various ways to pray the same thing: "Thy will be done." Torah refers to far more than the superficial idea of observing stop signs. It is, after all, the name of the first five books of the Old Testament, most of which narrates the *history* of God's dealings with his people. Torah has to do with people relating with God as was intended from creation, and thereby living a faithful, balanced, and whole life according to God's just and loving will. *Torah* is God's way of making people of God.

To get this idea across, the psalmist asks that his entire being be given over to doing God's will. "Seven times a day I praise thee for thy righteous ordinances" (164), meaning that *all* the day is given to walking in the way of the Lord. The word for *heart* is used fifteen times.* God's will is meant to be interiorized, to the point that it becomes the true source of one's joy and delight.† And it is also meant to be received and accomplished by one's entire body: lips, mouth, tongue, eyes, feet, hands, flesh.

No wonder the psalmist uses 176 verses and the entire Hebrew alphabet—beginning to end—to make this great prayer. "Thy will be done" is a prayer taught by the living and incarnate Torah of God—the Alpha and the Omega—who himself gave his entire being and all his days to the ways of God.

---

*   See, for example, Ps. 119:2, 11, 34, 58, 80, 112, 161.
†   See, for example, Ps. 119:14, 24, 47, 77, 92, 143, 174.

FROM THE FATHERS

The soul presses forward for a glimpse of hidden mysteries, to the very abode of the Word, and to his light and brightness. In that bosom and secret dwelling place of the Father, the soul hastens to hear his word.

Ambrose

Try reading Psalm 119 as if it were Jesus's prayer to his Father.

Then read it by inserting *Word* wherever *Torah* (law) and its synonyms appear.

See what further meaning such prayers might uncover.

25

Saturday of Lent III
PSALM 73

But for me it is good to be near God.

v. 28

I WANT YOU TO KNOW HOW TO STUDY THEOLOGY IN THE right way," wrote Martin Luther in the preface to a collection of his writings. "You should completely despair of your own sense and reason, for by these you will not attain the goal."[5] Formed by the monastic life, Luther knew the traditional method for engaging with the scriptures: *lectio, meditatio, oratio, contemplatio* (reading, meditation, prayer, contemplation). But to these he added one more step: *tentatio*—struggle. Though when he wrote this, Luther was teaching on another psalm (119), he may just as well have had Psalm 73 in mind.

Psalm 73 opens book three of the Psalter. As a wisdom psalm, it summarizes one of the central lessons of books one and two: personal blessing has nothing to do with wealth and success and everything to do with living in the presence of God. But, to reach this conclusion, the psalmist does not argue theological principles. Instead, he makes the honest and arduous struggle from faith, to questioning, to doubt, and back again to faith, all in a very public fashion. The opening verse, "Truly God is good to the upright," is presented both as a declaration of faith and as the leading question, "Is he really?" Almost immediately the psalmist's attention is turned to a contrary answer. What trips him up is the prosperity of the wicked, which he sees all around him (Ps. 73:3–5). In this struggle, he joins other great questioners in the Bible, like Job and Jeremiah. One of life's profoundest mysteries is presented once again: Why do the wicked prosper? (Jer. 12:1).

In the face of all the evidence—the success of the arrogant; their health and their wealth; their pride before others and even before God; not to mention that they are praised by people all around them—the psalmist begins to question the value of his own faithfulness. Is it all in vain to think that following God and his ways will bring me blessing when each day I know only pain? (Ps. 73:13–14). How am I to make sense of all this? He cannot, and so we reach the low point in the psalm.

The return from doubt to faith begins not with any change in circumstances but with the psalmist going "into the sanctuary of God" (17). There, in the presence of God, he begins to see the long view of things and something far more important than temporal blessing rises to the fore. Beginning with verse 21, the psalm is addressed directly to God, because here *with God*—held, guided, received by God—all other matters fall away.

In the end, the problem is not really solved and an answer is not found. We still do not know why the wicked are allowed to prosper as they do, nor why the innocent must suffer. It is sufficient, and "good," to be near God (28). One is reminded of another conversation about another mystery, also unsolvable. In that case, the "doubter" said much the same thing: "Lord, to whom shall we go? You have the words of eternal life" (John 6:68). Such profound theology can only be shaped by prayer . . . and struggle.

FROM THE FATHERS

You are my portion. You are abundant to me for all things. I have sought nothing but that I might possess you as my share. . . . Possessing nothing, I possess all things, because I possess Christ. . . . Therefore, possessing all things in him, I seek no other reward, because he is the reward of all.

Ambrose

If I am going to be honest with you, Lord,
I think that I am less concerned that the wicked prosper
    than that I do not.
Perhaps, then, to reach my goal,
I need to change where I've drawn the finish line.

26

Fourth Sunday of Lent
PSALM 135

Whatever the LORD pleases he does.

v. 6

TOGETHER WITH PSALM 136, PSALM 135 MAKES UP A song of praise known as the "Great Hallel." Among other places in the Jewish liturgy, it is traditionally sung at the conclusion of the Jewish Passover. The reason for this is made clear by the text: the psalmist is remembering both the divine call of Israel and God's intervening works of power and wonder in order to secure and preserve that call. In all likelihood, the psalm was written for use in the temple, probably in celebration of a festival of some kind.

The invitation to "Praise the Lord" (Hallelujah), which frames the psalm like a one-word antiphon, is joyfully addressed to those who "stand in the house of the LORD" (Ps. 135:2). There is nothing remotely introverted or meditative about this psalm. It reaches out with enthusiasm to all within earshot. With that aim, the Eastern Orthodox tradition appoints Psalms 135 and 136 to be used together at Matins on solemn feast days of the church. The psalmist introduces two themes that make this use especially appropriate. Verses 4 and 5 begin with the word *for*, giving the reasons why praise is to be offered. Both themes are fundamental to the identity of God's people, those formed by the old covenant and the new.

"For the LORD has chosen Jacob for himself" (4)—the first cause of our praise is *the call of God*. Were it not for God's choice of us, we would never know who God is in the first place. "We love, because he first loved us" (1 John 4:19). The same can be said about knowing God. Any knowledge we have of God is because God revealed himself to us. We did not find God. God found us. This is one of the cornerstones of Israel's identity (see Exod. 19:5–6; Deut. 7:6–8), and of new Israel's identity as well (see Rom. 1:7; 1 Cor. 1:2; 1 Pet. 1:2). The psalmist names this as the very first reason why those gathered in the temple should be praising God: *You are here because God wants you. He found you, like a needle in a haystack. He picked you up and took you home for his own. Praise the Lord!*

"For . . . the LORD is great, and . . . above all gods" (5)—the second reason for praise is *the salvation of God*. No one is more cognizant of God's mighty power than the one who has been saved by it. For the psalmist, the story of the delivery of Israel from Egypt is the primary example of God's saving strength, which cannot be limited or defeated. Neither is it arbitrary in its exercise. God wielded his power for the sake of his people—working signs and wonders, subduing their enemies, bringing them through the wilderness, leading them into a new land as he had promised. *Compare such deeds to what you get from the gold and silver idols you see around you. Made by human hands—maybe even your hands—can they even speak, much less act? There is only one Name worthy of your praise, and because you belong to him, you know who he is. Praise the Lord!*

FROM THE FATHERS

God is both Creator and Provider, and his power of creating, sustaining and providing is his good will. For "whatsoever the Lord pleased he has done, in heaven and on earth," and none resisted his will. He willed all things to be made, and they were made; he wills the world to endure, and it does endure; and all things whatsoever he wills are done.

John of Damascus

> *Neither of these reasons to praise you, Father,*
> *has anything to do with the condition of my heart,*
> *nor the condition of my day:*
> *You called me.*
> *You saved me.*
> *Praise the Lord!*

27

Monday of Lent IV
PSALM 70

O God, come to my assistance;
O Lord, make haste to help me.

v. 1*

I T IS QUITE PROBABLE THAT THE OPENING VERSE OF
Psalm 70 (which may also be found in Psalm 40:13) has been
prayed more in the last two thousand years than any other
line in the Psalter. In the Latin Vulgate it reads: *Deus, in adiutorium
meum intende; Domine, ad adiuvandum me festina*—"O God, come to my
assistance; O Lord, make haste to help me." In the sixth century,
Benedict of Nursia wrote a rule to govern life in his monastery, a
rule that eventually became the defining code for most of Western
monasticism. There he instructed that this verse be recited to
begin seven out of the eight daily prayer services of his monks
(see chapter 18 of the *Rule of St. Benedict*).The practice has been
going on ever since, not only in Benedictine monasteries but in
churches as well.

There is a sense of urgency that soaks through these brief verses,
is there not? The staccato-like style of the prayer seems to build

_____

* This Douay-Rheims translation, where it is called Psalm 69:2 because of
numbering differences, is the version used in many monastic breviaries.

in intensity until it reaches the final burst of the psalm: "Do not tarry!" (Ps. 70:5). There is no time for ornate poetry or carefully crafted stanzas. For the psalmist, it is not a steady current that carries his desires to God. His prayers ride on the rapids. This makes the repeated use of those opening lines in daily prayer all the more interesting.

Benedict took one of the most animated, if not agitated, lines of the psalms and made it the starting point for one of the most steady, if not monotonous, prayers of the church. He was drawing upon a much older tradition that found in this prayer the cry of every human heart. A century before Benedict's Rule, the verse was popular among the monks of the Egyptian desert whose entire lives were given to prayer. One of those monks, an old man by the name of Isaac, spoke of the importance of this prayer to a visitor. He advised his listener:

> This verse should be poured out in unceasing prayer so that we may be delivered in adversity and preserved and not puffed up in prosperity. You should, I say, meditate constantly on this verse in your heart. You should not stop repeating it when you are doing any kind of work or performing some service or are on a journey. . . . Let sleep overtake you as you meditate upon this verse until you are formed by having used it ceaselessly and are in the habit of repeating it even while asleep. Let this be the first thing that comes to you when you awake, let it anticipate every other thought as you get up, let it send you to your

knees as you arise from your bed, let it bring you from there to every work and activity, and let it accompany you at all times.[6]

FROM THE FATHERS

Not without reason has this verse been selected from out of the whole body of Scripture. For it takes up all the emotions that can be applied to human nature and, with great correctness and accuracy, it adjusts itself to every condition and every attack.

John Cassian

There is no better way to say it, Father.
I desperately need your help.
No one else can do it.
Please hurry!

28

Tuesday of Lent IV
PSALM 96

O sing to the LORD *a new song.*

v. 1

P SALM 96 IS AMONG THOSE RELATIVELY FEW PSALMS that contain only one theme. There is no prayer for deliverance from enemies; no lament for one's sickness or suffering; no cry for help in the midst of trial; no rehearsal of Israel's history; no proverbial teaching about following in the way of the Lord. A single chord is insistently struck again and again. And though the word *hallelujah* never appears in the psalm, we hear its sound in virtually every verse—*praise!*

The biblical record tells us the Levites sang Psalm 96 in celebration as David brought the ark to Jerusalem. The psalm as it appears in 1 Chronicles 16:23–33 matches the Psalter almost word for word. It is difficult for us to imagine the impassioned joy that would have accompanied this event. We see the ark as a historical artifact of the Israelites' journey to the Promised Land, but it was far more than an object. It was the divinely appointed sign of God's presence with his people. In many respects, it was what we would call a sacrament, for within its measurable physical dimensions it carried an immeasurable spiritual treasure. Its return signified God's own return, and its placement within the city of Jerusalem signified God's own enthronement as king over not only Israel but the whole world. "Say among the *nations*," cries the psalmist, "'The LORD reigns!'" (Ps. 96:10, emphasis added).

The psalmist calls for a "new song" because God's rule brings a new day. No melody from the "old" life will suffice. Despite the distance that separates them, heaven and earth, Jew and Gentile are called upon to sing in unison. The simple reason given is that God is *great* (4). He is superior to all others that might be called gods (5); he reigns over the entire world that he set into order (10); and he is the only one who can (and will) sit as judge with unwavering truthfulness and impeccable fairness. This was the new order of things envisioned by the seer of Revelation, who also *heard* the vision in a new song sung to the Lamb (Rev. 5:3). A new creation will require a new sound.

As a liturgical prayer of the church, Psalm 96 has most often been sung in connection with Christmas and Easter. It is easy to see why. The coming One, who will reign as King of kings, came first as Servant of servants. Masked by fragile infant flesh, he nevertheless entered the world accompanied by his courtiers of honor, majesty, strength, and beauty (Ps. 96:6). If angel witnesses greeted his birth with "Glory to God!" then all the peoples of the earth together with the earth itself (1) cannot stand quiet—there can be no such thing as mute witnesses to the salvation of God (2). The psalm's use at Easter is equally fitting. There is no work more marvelous to be declared among the nations than the glory of the Lord's resurrection (3). The risen One, who now reigns as Lord of lords, and through whom all things in heaven and on earth were made (John 1:3), raised all of creation with him. Even the trees of the wood—and the wood of the Tree—sing for joy before the Lord.

FROM THE FATHERS
When the whole earth sings a new song, it is the house of God. It is built by singing, its foundations are believing, it is erected by hoping, it is completed by loving.

Augustine

Sometime today, Lord, I must praise you.
For the new creation that I now live in actually lives in me.
So, sometime today, Lord, I will praise you.

29

Wednesday of Lent IV
PSALM 120

Deliver me, O LORD, from lying lips.

v. 2

P SALM 120 IS THE FIRST OF A GROUP OF FIFTEEN PSALMS, each of which is entitled "A Song of Ascents." They form a "psalter within the Psalter" and are worth reading as a whole. It is thought that these psalms may have been used by worshipers making their pilgrimage to Zion in observance of one of the great festivals of the Jewish year. A further look at these fifteen psalms reveals that they can be divided into five groups of three, each group having its own particular emphasis.

The first two groups deal with troubles brought by external threats and pressures. The psalmist complains about his suffering, but also looks to God's intervention and is confident in God's righteousness and strength. Zion itself, the City of God, is seen as the pivot point for all of the Lord's dealings with his people. The third group of psalms takes a more philosophical approach, with little said about God's forgiveness or salvation. They read more like proverbs with an emphasis on home and family life. The fourth group returns to an intensely personal expression of prayer, especially of lament and petition, calling for the exercise of that most difficult of virtues—patience. The last group focuses on God's purposeful election of Zion—the people with whom he has made a covenant, and his chosen dwelling place.

Psalm 120, therefore, becomes the preface for this little volume of prayers. In an almost matter-of-fact manner, the psalmist records: When I was in trouble, I called upon the Lord, and he heard me (Ps. 120:1). This is the way he lives with his God day to day, step by step. But those steps are impeded by enemies—by lying lips and deceitful tongues (2). There are no more damaging weapons to undermine the progress of the saint than duplicity and deceit. And what better instrument than the tongue? In a lying tongue the psalmist sees, on the one hand, the deadly accuracy of a razor-pointed arrow and, on the other, the uncontainable destructive power of fire. (Wood from the broom tree was known to burn with an especially intense heat and its roots were used to produce charcoal.) The Letter of James says, "How great a forest is set ablaze by a small fire"—and the tongue *is* that fire! (see Jas. 3:5–12).

Assailed by such harmful forces, the psalmist likens his distress to being separated from his beloved homeland, exiled from the City of God. He imagines living in Meshech, a warring nation from Asia Minor near the Black Sea (Ezek. 38:2), and with Kedar, a desert tribe from north Arabia, thought to be descendants of Ishmael (Isa. 21:17; Gen. 25:13). These situations represent the worst imaginable condition for the pilgrim—separation from fellow travelers, isolation from family. Against this possibility, the psalmist makes his daily cry, "Deliver me, O LORD." Is this not an appropriate prayer for all who make their pilgrimage along rough terrain, as they make their way up to the New Jerusalem?

FROM THE FATHERS

Kedar means darkness, and darkness stands for this present world for, we are told, "the light shines in the darkness; and the darkness comprehends it not."

Jerome

Lord, if I am to ask you to "save me from lying lips,"
    then let's first start with my own.
May the arrows shot at me—and by me—never find their mark.

30

Thursday of Lent IV
PSALM 116

I love the LORD, *because he has heard my voice.*

v. 1

T HE SPIRIT OF PSALM 116 RECALLS THE PUBLIC INVITATION delivered by another psalmist: "Come and hear, all you who fear God, and I will tell what he has done for me" (Ps. 66:16). This author is telling forth, "in the presence of all his people" (Ps. 116:14, 18), what God has done for him. For an act of deliverance that "delivered my soul from death" (8), he is returning thanks to God, not in the privacy of his prayer closet but in the very public setting of the temple. This is the song of one who, having called upon God in lonely desperation, is now calling upon him with unconcealed worship and praise.

As a public declaration, the opening phrase, "I love the LORD," is almost unique. Only Psalm 18 begins similarly, "I love thee, O LORD," though it uses a different word for *love*. So often we hear the psalms speak of praising, thanking, and extolling; and of complaining, pleading, and lamenting. We know immediately that we are in for something different when the psalmist begins by revealing a corner of his own heart. His experience of salvation is part of a larger tapestry, an intimate relationship with the Almighty threaded with love as well as trust.

The exact nature of the psalmist's predicament is unknown. It appears it brought him to the very brink of death (3); and that he was helpless to do anything about it other than to beseech the Lord for deliverance (4). The joy he now feels as he stands before the congregation and makes his thanksgiving sacrifice is founded upon what God has done for him, first by *hearing* the sound of his prayer and, second, by *answering* him with mercy and help. Heaven's listening ears, the psalmist now knows, are always inclined toward the cries of the "simple" (6)—in Hebrew, the young and inexperienced, both in age and in condition—and especially toward those who are "dying" (15). As John Calvin put it in his commentary on this psalm, "God does not hold his servants in so little estimation as to expose them to death casually."[7]

God's ability to save is no longer a matter of faith for the poet. He *knows* that God answers prayer. The only worthy response he can give is to fulfill the promises he made when he was in distress: he will call upon God for the rest of his life (2); walk in the ways of the Lord all the days of his life (9); and go to the sanctuary of God where, in the sight of all God's people, he will give testimony to what God has done by offering a sacrifice of thanksgiving (17–18). No wonder this psalm and its "cup of salvation" (13) have come to be used at the heart of both Jewish and Christian worship: as one of the Hallel psalms at the time of Passover, in celebration of the Exodus; and on Holy Thursday at the Eucharist, in celebration of salvation in Jesus Christ.

FROM THE FATHERS

I have loved God, who is the highest of objects to be desired, and I have received with joy sufferings for his sake. . . . [T]he pangs of death, the dangers of hell, the affliction, the pain, all things whatsoever are desirable to him because of the love of God. . . . These words seem to have equal weight with the words of the apostle and to be spoken by him with the same feeling: "Who shall separate us from the love of Christ?"

Basil the Great

What would my prayer be, Lord,
    if I could sum up all my prayers in a word?
Would it—
    will it—
        ever be
            love?

31

Friday of Lent IV

PSALM 142

Thou art my refuge, my portion in the land of the living.

v. 5

T HE CRY OF THE POET IN PSALM 142 IS DIRECTED TO his only hope in a time of loneliness and faintheartedness. The superscription attached to this psalm suggests that it was written by David "when he was in the cave." The exact circumstances are unclear, but the two incidences we have recorded in Scripture of David in a cave—1 Samuel 22:1 and 1 Samuel 24:3–4—are related to the time when he was fleeing for his life from a jealous and vengeful King Saul. Most praying this psalm are not in such dire conditions, though even today in many parts of the world faith in God is lived at the risk of losing everything dear, even one's own life. We can pray these desperate words at any time in the name of those who suffer such persecution.

On a more personal level, there are at least two significant elements of this psalm that anyone can understand. The first is the utter sense of *loneliness*, of abandonment even. Not only is the psalmist in trouble but no one cares. He looks for consolation,

for someone to offer compassion and reassurance, and is bereft
of all good company. "There is none who takes notice of me,"
he laments, adding "no man cares for me" (Ps. 142:4). One translation reads, "There was no patron for my soul"—no advocate,
no ally. However independent and self-sufficient we may consider
ourselves to be, the human heart recoils in grief at such times of
loneliness. In such bitter times the heart yearns for a companion.

A second place we can all perhaps relate to is found in verse 3
(emphasis added): "When my spirit is *faint*." The word appears eight
other times in the psalms, referring variously to the psalmist's heart,
flesh, soul, or spirit. In other words, he says: I am so tired—in body,
mind, and spirit—that I don't think I can go on. If one's heart can be
bone-tired, that is what this word means. For the psalmist, a brisk
walk in the way of the Lord has reverted to a tenuous shuffling.
His fears make each step slow, and his loneliness makes each step
uncertain.

In fact, however, the psalmist *does* have company in his condition. Despite his fear, he knows that there *is* one who knows his
path, one who hears his cry (6). For the psalmist, this is no theological platitude. Placing hope in the Lord is the utter conviction
of his heart. There is nowhere else to turn and, notwithstanding
his vacillation between despair and trust, he expects God to bring
his soul "out of prison" (7). The psalmist uses an interesting word
when he describes the Lord as his "portion in the land of the living"
(5). It is the same Hebrew word used to refer to the inheritance
of land apportioned to each of the twelve tribes of Israel. In other
words, like one who lives off the land, the psalmist "lives off" God.
With such bountiful provision at hand, the psalmist expects that

the Lord will renew his strength, so that, now surrounded by the heartening company of the righteous (7), he will once again "walk and not faint" (Isa. 40:31).

FROM THE FATHERS

Now when the enemy of righteousness, the foe of the human race, . . . that is to say, Satan, the opponent of all virtues, and the hater of the upright life of the children of humankind, saw that this brother was overcoming and bringing to naught all his crafty designs by the might of his simple obedience . . . he made a plan to lay snares for him in the path of his spiritual excellence.

Palladius

> *Only you know the path that is set before me, Father.*
> *So, when it is desolate, and when it is dangerous,*
> *—and when I am dog-tired—*
> *you need to be the first one I turn to.*

32

Saturday of Lent IV
PSALM 4

In peace I will both lie down and sleep.

v. 8

THOUGH IT BEGINS WITH AN APPEAL FOR HELP, Psalm 4 rings with an unmistakable tone of confidence throughout. Even the initial petition of verse 1, "Answer me when I call, O God of my right!" (literally, my "defense attorney"), is followed immediately with the bold assertion: you have given me space whenever I've been in a tight spot. The psalmist's condition is sometimes translated as *anguish*, which comes from a Latin word meaning narrowness or tightness. Who cannot appreciate this description of one's state of mind when pain or trouble suffocates all the senses? Though the psalmist feels trapped, he draws immediately upon his past experiences of relief. His prayer is made with the unwavering certainty that he will once again be set free.

The psalmist then turns to addressing two sets of people. In verses 2–3, he speaks directly to his enemies. When he asks them how long they will lie in order to slander him, he is not so much complaining as mocking. In other words: Why are you wasting your breath? Why are you boxing at the air? You cannot harm me, he declares, because you cannot reach me. Like all those who call him Lord, I have been set apart in a safe place by God himself. Hidden in that place, my words will reach God, and your disparaging words cannot reach me.

In verses 4–7, the psalmist turns to his disheartened listeners; we can safely assume they are disheartened because of the advice he gives to them. They seem to be caught in the same tight place as is the psalmist, so he takes it upon himself to show them the way out. First, he tells them, do not let anger at your adversaries lead you into sin. As a student of the psalms, Paul draws upon this advice when he writes to the Ephesians: "Be angry but do not sin; do not let the sun go down on your anger, and give no opportunity to the devil" (Eph. 4:26–27). It is fine to be angry with those wantonly seeking to harm you, but do not let your anger turn to resentment and bitterness. Above all, do not let it ignite into revenge. Second, be quiet. Go to your bed and silently "commune with your own hearts" (Ps. 4:4). Before God, take stock of your condition, quietly ponder what you know to be true, and remind yourself of what God has already done. Third, when you rise, go to the temple and bring true worship ("right sacrifices") to the Lord. There, in the setting of the covenant, fulfill your duties to God. Finally, "put your trust in the LORD" (5).

Do not sin; be still; pray privately and corporately (both are intimately related and required in this psalm); trust in God. This is the wise advice rooted in the psalmist's own testimony. Even under duress, he has more joy knowing that God is with him than if he had all the possessions in the world. In that blessed condition, he can go to bed with a peaceful heart and a clear conscience, which is the best elixir for a good night's sleep. Is it any wonder that Benedict directed his monks to sing this psalm at the closing prayer of every day (*Rule of Benedict* 18.19)?

FROM THE FATHERS

Nothing, you see, is so calculated to bring peace as knowledge of God and possession of virtue, banishing afar conflict of the passions and not allowing one to be at odds with oneself. . . . Righteous persons . . . in their waking hours enjoy life, and in nighttime take their rest with great satisfaction.

John Chrysostom

No other peace
  —neither with others, nor with circumstances—
  can make up for any unrest with you, Father.
Am I skirmishing with you anywhere?

33

Fifth Sunday of Lent
PSALM 92

It is good to give thanks to the LORD,
to sing praises to thy name, O Most High.

v. 1

CCORDING TO RABBINIC TEACHING, THIS HYMN was sung in the temple on the Sabbath during the time of the morning sacrifice. As the new day was welcomed and the offering was being made by the priest, the choir would chant: "It is good to give thanks to the LORD." This worshipful declaration of the early morning was meant to set the tone for the whole coming day, and into the night (Ps. 92:2). Morning to evening, sunrise to sunset, birth to death—declaring God's steadfast love and faithfulness is the lifelong, "good" song to be carried by every believer so long as there is breath to sing. (And even after the last note is sounded, a new song will be sung with the coming New Sabbath [Rev. 5:9]!) Psalm 103 calls for all *things* to praise God; this psalm calls for singing God's praises at all *times*.

From the psalmist's point of view, and perhaps drawing upon his own experience, this especially includes those times when it appears that God's ways are being thwarted. The wickedness of men, he seems to be saying, in no way diminishes the faithfulness of God. It requires wisdom to understand this—in other words, it requires seeing things from God's point of view—but the prosperity of the ungodly is short-lived (Ps. 92:6–7). For a time, it may appear that injustice is prevailing, but only a "fool" would think that this is the whole story. From heaven's perspective of time, what seems to last forever is really as transient as the fading grass (see Ps. 102:4, 11; Isa. 37:27).

What *will* last, most certainly, are the lives of the righteous. No doubt this is why, in addition to being used in the morning, Psalm 92 came to be sung in monasteries for the celebration of martyrs' feast days. "Premature" as their deaths seem to have been, those who faithfully "sang" their love of God to the point of sacrifice, sing on. The sound of their testimony still echoes off the walls of Christ's church. Such is true for all who are rooted in God (Ps. 92:13). Unlike the grass, their lives are perennial, like the elegant fruit-bearing date palms and strong majestic cedars. Their leaves never whither (recall Ps. 1:3). Standing tall and graceful in the house of God, they flourish with praise, *always*. The vitality of their witness actually strengthens with the passing of time. The older they get, the sweeter grows their fruit. Their very presence, night and day, declares the truth and righteousness of God (Ps. 92:15).

FROM THE FATHERS

An old man used to say, "It is written, 'The righteous one shall blossom like the palm tree.' Now these words make known that the soul acquires height, and straightness of stature, and sweetness from beautiful deeds. But there is another quality that is found in the palm, that is, a single, white heart, which is wholly suitable both for work (or useful for being worked). And this must be found in the righteous person, for his heart must be single and simple, and it must be accustomed to look toward God only."

From the Desert Fathers

Lord, clear the smoke from my eyes,
that keeps me from seeing things as they truly are;
that keeps me from seeing you as you truly are.
Then, clear the catch in my throat,
that keeps me from giving you thanks,
that keeps me from praising your name,
forever.

34

Monday of Lent V
PSALM 13

How long, O LORD?
Wilt thou forget me for ever?

v. 1

THE AUTHOR OF PSALM 13 BEGINS BY VOICING the classic question eventually raised by anyone who believes in a loving God: "How long, O LORD?" The urgency of tone is matched by the insistent repetition: How long will you forget me? How long will you ignore me? How long will I be in pain? How long will my enemies prosper while I know only suffering? In the world of childish impatience, these would be the questions of one who knows nothing of time and distance: "How long till we get there?" But these are not the questions of an uncomfortable child. The psalmist's suffering is real. It is difficult enough that his heart is "vexed" (as it is rendered in Coverdale's translation*) and his soul is in pain. His condition is made more difficult because of the taunts of his enemies. The success of those who hate him make his

---

* Myles Coverdale's version of the Psalms was used in the Episcopal Church's BCP until 1979.

own diminishment all the more bitter: *My enemy prospers while I languish and, worst of all, he is happy about it.*

The triumph of his enemy is not the cause of the psalmist's worst agitation. He begins his poem lamenting his seeming inability to get through to God. *Where is God when I need him?* he asks. *It seems he has forgotten me. Even if I look for him, he hides himself from my sight. Unless things change somehow, I will die feeling this way. What could be worse? How long is this going to go on?* The anxiety that accompanies such emptiness weighs like the stillness of a bone-chilling fog on the human soul. Feeling yourself abandoned is one of the darkest and coldest of sufferings. In such a prayer as this, you can rightly hear Jesus crying out to his Father in the Garden of Gethsemane. The night is closing in, the enemy is advancing, the "sleep of death" awaits.

This sense of God's absence in a time of trouble is a deep and painful mystery that cannot be explained by reason or platitude. Equally mysterious is the sense of return to trust and faith. Like other lament psalms, Psalm 13 turns on a dime with two tiny words: "But I" (see also Ps. 31:14; Ps. 59:16; Ps. 71:14). What explains the psalmist's abrupt change of tone: "My heart shall rejoice in thy salvation"? (Ps. 13:5). As in the case of so many of the psalms of "complaint," it is almost as if the very act of crying out to God for help inspires renewed faith and confidence. Having begun in despair, the final note struck by most of these psalms is one of hope, even of joy: "I will praise the Name of the Lord Most Highest" (Ps. 13:6, BCP). Like the mystery that takes us from Gethsemane's garden to the garden tomb, Psalm 13 (in just six short verses!) takes us from the deepest loneliness to the highest joy. This, eventually, is the journey of every disciple who "takes up the cross" and follows Jesus (Lk. 9:23).

FROM THE FATHERS

Just as when God defends us and stands by us, everything damaging is removed from us, so when he keeps his distance and forgets us, our soul is cut in two, our heart plunged in sorrow, those who do harm fall on us and life becomes craggy and precipitous. Now this is allowed to happen for our advantage so that [we] may be goaded into being more zealous. . . . And so, even abandonment by God is a form of providence.

John Chrysostom

There is nothing more frightening to me, Father, than the loss of you.
I know, there are many other losses that I seem to fear more.
But in truth, they can all be endured if you remember me.
But if you should forget me, there would be nothing left to lose.

35

Tuesday of Lent V
PSALM 18

I love thee, O LORD, my strength.

v. 1

A
ND DAVID SPOKE TO THE LORD THE WORDS OF THIS
song on the day when the LORD delivered him from
the hand of all his enemies, and from the hand of Saul"
(2 Samuel 22:1). In this way the writer of Israel's history introduces
a song of David that is added later to a larger collection of songs
(psalms) and becomes what we now know as Psalm 18. Save for an
opening declaration added in the Psalm 18 version—"I love thee,
O LORD, my strength"—the verses of Psalm 18 and 2 Samuel 22
are virtually identical.

It is not clear whether David composed the song in the flush of
a specific victory over an enemy (particularly Saul), or at a time
much later in life as he reflected back upon the many battles and
sufferings he had endured. What is clear, however, is that this
is the vibrant and grateful testimony of one whose enemies had
surrounded him threatening destruction, whose soul had been
entangled in the cords of the underworld and the "snares of death"

(Ps. 18:5), and whose life had been saved by the prevailing power
of God.

In some respects, without the words of verse 6, there might be
no testimony at all: "In my distress I called upon the LORD . . . he
heard my voice, and my cry to him reached his ears." The rest
of the song records the deliverance experienced by the psalmist
after he calls out—even *complained*—to his God. In a state of utter
helplessness, he turns to the Lord his rock. From that point on
things happen fast: the earth trembles, the heavens bow down,
the lightning flashes, the thunder rolls. The best way that the
psalmist can describe his miraculous salvation is with the poetry
of power.

"While we were still weak, at the right time Christ died for the
ungodly" (Rom. 5:6). The saving power of God, openly displayed
through the bursting skies or quietly hidden within the shadow
of the cross, is always wielded on behalf of the weak and needy.
It is a strength that can never be overcome by its enemies. The
psalmist is sure of this truth—"I love thee, O LORD, my strength."
His very breath is a testimony to God's salvation. Therefore, he is
determined to keep the ways of God (Ps. 18:23) and to sing the
praise of God (Ps. 18:49) all the days of his life.

FROM THE FATHERS

Take care not to let trust in your own strength steal on you, for
you are human, and "cursed by everyone who puts his hope in
man" (Jer. 17:5). But put your trust fully and with your whole
heart in God, and he will be your strength; trust him lovingly and
gratefully and say to him humbly and faithfully, "I will love you,

O Lord, my strength," because that very love of God, when it is perfected in us, "casts out fear" (1 John. 4:18).

Augustine

God, I know your delivering power in my life.
   I have felt the grip of your hand,
   the force of your arm,
   the strength of your shoulders—
      when you caught me,
      when you held me,
         when you carried me.
I need to know that power today, Lord.
Reach down from on high, and take hold of me again.

36

Wednesday of Lent V
PSALM 30

O Lord my God,
I will give thanks to thee for ever.
v. 12

USING THE IMAGERY OF NIGHT AND DAY—OF mourning and dancing—the poet of Psalm 30 takes his readers on a flashback journey through some of his life's lowest lows and highest highs. He recounts occasions of desperation, of God's delivering power, of good health and prosperity, of crumbling hopes, of the bleak sense of God's absence, and finally, of full restoration to wholeness and joy. He tells us that all of these ups and downs occur under the thoughtful care of the Almighty and that, in the end, the only suitable response he can make is to give thanks to the Lord his God.

The opening verses describe critical low points in light of God's saving help. Apparently the psalmist faced danger from both without and within. He suffered a nearly lethal blow in an attack from his enemies, and mortal illness came close to taking the breath from his body. He was downcast—at the very threshold of death and hell. But each of these nocturnal woes was followed by a new dawn of gladness. He happily recalls that in the morning light's brightness, the darkness of the night seemed to have lasted only moments. The joy that comes in the morning is more than restorative—it is heaven's healing amnesiac. "For this slight momentary affliction," echoes Paul, "is preparing for us an eternal weight of glory" (2 Cor. 4:17).

Rescued and recuperated, the psalmist takes his well-being and good fortune for granted. He admits that, from the carefree vantage point of his hilltop, he has forgotten the source of his health and prosperity. In Psalm 10, we are told the wicked boast they will never suffer adversity. Why is it that, when good things happen, we so quickly forget the Giver of all good, and when bad things happen, we so quickly "remember" him with our incriminating, "Why are *you* doing this to me?"

Suddenly, for this psalmist, everything collapses and it is as if God had departed from him. "Then cried I unto thee, O LORD; I gat me to my Lord *right humbly*" (Ps. 30:8, BCP, emphasis added). God's answer to this penitent cry is to once again lift the soul of his servant out from under pain's unbearable weight, and to reclothe him in garments of salvation (see Isa. 61:10). The psalmist's response to God is to once again give thanks—this time "without ceasing" (Ps. 30:13, BCP).

FROM THE FATHERS

The joy of God is not found in just any soul, but, if someone has mourned much and deeply his own sin . . . as if bewailing his own death, the mourning of such a one is turned into joy. . . . The mourning garment, which he put on when bewailing his sin, is torn, and the tunic of joy is placed around him, and the cloak of salvation.

Basil the Great

Father, I have known your delivering power
    more times than I can number.
There seems no end to your patience,
    just as there seems no end to my need.
Hear me once again, as, in the dark of night,
    I cry to you for help.
And hear me once again, as, in the morning light,
    I give thanks to you for your mercy.

37

Thursday of Lent V
PSALM 55

Cast your burden on the LORD, and he will sustain you;
he will never permit the righteous to be moved.

v. 22

OMMENTATORS ON THE PSALMS AS EARLY AS
Athanasius in the fourth century have observed that they
give utterance in prayer to every conceivable human
sentiment and emotion. Psalm 55 expresses one of the most
universal among them: the longing to run away from all pain and
suffering. It is the most natural reaction in the world, and the poet
captures the desire in language of flight and escape: "O that I had
wings like a dove! I would fly away and be at rest" (Ps. 55:6). What
one of us has not imagined successfully escaping the "raging wind
and tempest" (8) of life's sometimes crushing circumstances? If
it were possible, would we not "make haste to escape" (Ps. 55:8,
BCP) and remain a safe distance from all that disquiets us? In the
face of his fear and trouble, the poet simply imagines himself to
be somewhere else, but in the end he realizes that this is not to
be. He cannot hide. His fervent prayer, therefore, is that God not
hide from him (1).

What causes the psalmist such grief and anguish? We come to realize it is not the usual pain of suffering at the hands of an enemy. Were that the case, he says, he could have borne it (12). No, this is the sharpest hurt of all: the betrayal of a friend—and not just an ordinary friend but a "familiar friend," a "companion," what Psalm 41 (see #13 above) tenderly calls a "bosom friend." The psalm reveals that theirs was a friendship with much shared in common, built upon a mutual love for the things of God (14). No wonder the blow leveled against the psalmist strikes so deep in his soul. No wonder he would like most of all to run from it. It is the destructive blow of treachery and deceit.

These verses describe the treachery experienced by Jesus at the hands of Judas, a treachery so central to Christ's passion that the apostle Paul summarizes the evening of the Lord's Supper as "the night when he was betrayed" (1 Cor. 11:23). There were many other horrific events that night, but they were all set in motion by the bitter kiss of a friend.

The verses of Psalm 55, therefore, go back and forth between describing the betrayer's faith*less*ness and God's faith*ful*ness. "There are friends who pretend to be friends," says the writer of Proverbs, "but there is a friend who sticks closer than a brother" (Prov. 18:24). It is to this eternal Friend that the psalmist turns in his confusion: "He who is enthroned from of old" will hear me (Ps. 55:19). And his hope is not disappointed. In the end, though he has been tripped up by the treachery of a friend, the Lord will bear up his burdened soul, and the souls of all who put their trust in him (22).

FROM THE FATHERS

If you believe that God makes provision for you, why be anxious or concerned about temporal affairs and the needs of your flesh? But if you do not believe that God makes provision for you, and for this reason you take pains to provide for your need separately from him, then you are the most wretched of all men. Why even be alive or go on living in such a case? "Cast your care upon the Lord, and he will nourish you."

Isaac of Nineveh

Father, let me never despair so much in my feelings of betrayal
that I grow numb to the betrayer in my own heart.
May my soul never be dried from tears of repentance
for the false kisses I have given you.

38

Friday of Lent V
PSALM 29

Ascribe to the LORD the glory of his name.

v. 2

PSALM 29 IS ONE OF THE LESSER-KNOWN PSALMS OF David. It is a call to worship the God who is "enthroned as king for ever" (Ps. 29:10)—the God who does scary things in the natural world and then assures us, as he assured his disciples in an about-to-be-capsized boat on the Sea of Galilee— the God who "bless[es] his people with peace" (11). But this call to worship is not addressed to us. It is addressed to God's "heavenly beings"—the angels. We are evidently meant to overhear and, like the seer of the book of Revelation, to join in. The psalmist tells us that, when we give God praise, we are seeing life from a heavenly perspective.

The poetry of Psalm 29 fuses together two worlds—the natural and the spiritual. The realms are related to one another and both are venues for the manifestation of God's glory. By discerning and then describing the presence of the invisible God within visible creation—in this case, a violent thunderstorm—the psalmist unveils for us the deeper meaning behind the forces of nature.

After calling upon all the supernatural authorities of heaven—angels, archangels, dominions, and powers—to render God worship and praise (1–2), the writer launches into a description of an approaching storm. Scholars tell us that the psalm is an accurate depiction of what takes place. The thunder begins to rumble over the Mediterranean Sea as dark clouds gather and the winds begin to howl. In short order the storm rages over land and even the strong cedars of Lebanon are no match for its violent winds. The mountains and hills themselves seem to shake and dance in turmoil. Then, the lightening—"flames of fire"—takes its toll (7). As if collaborating with the incessant wind, its flashes strip the trees of their branches and terrify the mother deer into prematurely calving. The power of the storm is irresistible.

In this psalm, the word for "thunder" and the word for "voice" are the same. The psalmist hears more than the clap of thunder and the strike of lightening in the storm. This is none other than the voice of God moving through all the land. In this "temple," under the canopy of a blazing sky, everything cries, "Glory to God." So it is that our hearts and voices are in heaven with the angels, crying, "Glory!" (9). Our trust is above the storm, where we know that this powerful God is in charge of our lives. There is no need for us to fear.

FROM THE FATHERS

"The voice of the Lord is over the waters." This verse forecasts the voice emanating from heaven at the Jordan River, "This is my Son, the Beloved, in whom I am well pleased." [The psalmist] called it "thunder" as coursing to the whole world through the sacred Gospels.

Theodoret of Cyr

> *I think that I would prefer the still, small voice,*
> > *the gentle whisper,*
> > *the quiet sound.*
> *But if the thunder is the only way to open my ears,*
> > *and thus to open my heart,*
> *Then thunder is welcome.*
> *Your silence is not an acceptable alternative.*
> *I'd rather be shaken,*
> > *than left alone.*

39

Saturday of Lent V
PSALM 76

Glorious art thou, more majestic
than the everlasting mountains.

v. 4

PSALM 76 IS IN PRAISE OF ZION, GOD'S DWELLING
place in Jerusalem. There, says the psalmist, God made his
stand against all his enemies and defeated them. There, all
of the weapons of war brought to bear against the City of God
were broken, hostile armies were vanquished, and opposing kings
were cut down. More glorious and enduring is Mount Zion than
all of the mountains that surround it.

The language and form of this psalm seem to indicate that it
was written during the time of the Babylonian Exile (sixth century
BCE). In other words, when this song was first sung, Jerusalem actually lay in ruins and its people were being held in captivity. What
reality does the psalmist see upon which he can make such claims?
Perhaps the same "reality" that inspired the apostle Paul to declare,
"No, in all these things we are more than conquerors through him
who loved us" (Rom. 8:37).

One of the earliest theologies of redemption saw God's saving work in Christ as a cosmic combat against sin, death, and the devil. Jesus came to do battle on our behalf, and his weapon was the Cross. Isn't the Lord's death and resurrection a precise picture of God's "dwelling place" ("The Word became flesh and dwelt among us") in ruins, sealed in the darkness of a tomb, ready to decay to dust and ashes? Yet, even the most powerful empire on earth at the time could not stand firm "when God *arose* to establish judgment" (Psalm 76:9, emphasis added). We might think of the soldiers at the tomb when we read that "the stouthearted were stripped of their spoil; they sank into sleep; all the men of war were unable to use their hands" (5).

The second verse of the psalm offers an interesting image. The psalmist uses two words to describe the temple when he says God is in Zion, translated as *abode* and *dwelling place*. But these words could just as easily be rendered as *hut* and *den*, referring to the lair of a lion. Did the psalmist intend to point us to the Lion of Judah, the conqueror of all rival princes and kings?

Psalm 76 is not a familiar nor oft-quoted psalm for most of us. Nevertheless, and particularly as we near the Feast of Feasts, these words can remind us that, when we stand at the baptismal font on the night of the Paschal Vigil, and once again renounce the devil and all his ways, we do so in the name of the One who is "glorious" (4) and victorious over all.

FROM THE FATHERS

I have found support in those who care nothing for this present life, but await the enjoyment of everlasting blessings, and these furnish me with manifold consolation. . . . [T]he truth of the divine Gospel has been publicly proclaimed and I, for my part, exclaim with the blessed [psalmist]: "Blessed be the Lord who alone does wondrous things."

Theodoret of Cyr

In any night's darkness, Father,
  I can sing with hope the song of the Night of nights:
"This is the night when Jesus Christ broke the chains of death
And rose triumphant from the grave.
Christ has conquered! Darkness vanishes forever!"

40

Palm Sunday /
Sunday of the Passion
PSALM 118

Blessed be he who enters in the name of the LORD!
We bless you from the house of the LORD.

v. 26

SALM 118 BELONGS TO A COLLECTION OF PSALMS
that have been categorized in Jewish tradition as "songs
of thanksgiving." (Other examples are Pss. 65, 67, 92,
and 107.) It is also the last of the great Hallel psalms (113–118)
sung at every major Jewish festival. These psalms give praise to
God by recounting a specific experience of his delivering power
or by remembering his gracious provision in times of need. The
happiness they express is like a musical sigh of relief: "Look at the
trouble I was in, and look what you, O Lord, did for me!" Only a
song of praise is suitable on such occasions.

The interesting thing about Psalm 118 is that, over time, it grew
into more than a personal testimony—it became the song of an
entire congregation in procession to the house of God. It became
an entire service of worship. At first, the psalmist may have
intended only to sing of how the Lord had heard him when he was

in trouble (Ps. 118:5). Perhaps this was the voice of the king after returning from battle. When he was surrounded by his enemies and it looked as if all was lost (11) he called upon the Lord and he was saved. "The LORD helped me," he thankfully declares (13).

Now, envision an assembly of worshipers approaching the temple. Someone is leading them and telling the same story of God's deliverance. In the beginning, they all respond to his call to give thanks with the phrase "His steadfast love endures for ever" (1–4); then they just walk and listen (5–18). A single voice proclaims the delivering power of God, even over death. Eventually they reach the door of the temple: "Open to me the gates of righteousness," the cantor calls out (19). The whole group is granted access and begins moving to the altar (21–25). There, they are welcomed by the priest: "Blessed be he who enters in the name of the LORD" (26), and they offer their sacrifice of thanksgiving (27–29). One poet's prayer has become an entire people's praise.

So it is that Psalm 118 made its way into Christian worship as the favored psalm for every Lord's Day celebration—every so-called "little Easter" of the liturgical year. The church has always heard the voice of the risen Christ in the testimony of the psalmist: "I shall not die, but I shall live" (17); as well as in the exuberant response of God's people: "The LORD is God, and he has given us light!" (27). The rejected stone, upon which all salvation is built (see Mk. 12:10–11), is none other than "he who enters in the name of the LORD" (26). In bread and wine, he is welcomed at the altar, and with cries of "Hosanna" ("Save us," Heb. *Hoshiah-na*) (25), he is welcomed into the gates of the heart.

FROM THE FATHERS

After the long centuries of dreadful night, the eternal day, our Christ, shone forth. The world had long awaited the splendor of his dawning. . . . The blessed psalmist saw this day in spirit when he sang, "This is the day the Lord has made; let us rejoice and be glad in it." Consequently, the apostle, too, calls believers children of light and of faith: "You are children of the light and children of the day" (1 Thess. 5:5).

Peter Chrysologus

You sometimes come unbidden to the gates of my heart, Lord,
bringing a light brighter than a thousand suns.
There you seek entry . . . and welcome . . .
and there I sometimes hold fast . . .
or bless your coming.

41

Monday of Holy Week

PSALM 80

Give ear, O Shepherd of Israel.

v. 1

PSALM 80 IS AN URGENT PLEA FOR HELP IN THE FACE of overwhelming destruction. And "destruction" is not too strong a word to describe the circumstances. This psalm may have been written at the time of the Assyrian conquest of the northern kingdom of Israel (about 722 BCE). In other words, a nation that had been created by God's design and inhabited by a people covenanted to him—a sign of God's handiwork on earth—was no more. Faced with such a tragic reversal of what had seemed to be God's fixed plan, what does the psalmist pray? What do any of us pray at such times, when the promises of God have "failed" and our dreams are falling like ash? Consider a few elements in this psalm that may guide us.

First, there is no mistaking the sense of urgency in the psalmist's words. Note the many imperatives which pour out of the psalmist's mouth—five of them in the opening three verses: give ear, shine forth, stir up, come, save us. (By the way, verse 2 is the inspiration behind the familiar sixteenth-century prayer for the first Sunday of Advent: "Stir up your power, O Lord, and with great might come among us.") Almost as quickly, they keep coming: restore us, turn again, have regard, look down, give us life! True need has no time to beat around the bush. The psalmist is not ashamed to insist that God do something, and do it soon.

Second, consider two images the psalmist uses to portray what God has already done for his people: God as the Shepherd of Israel, and Israel as the Vine in God's vineyard. Together they make for a rather mixed metaphor, but when one is in pain, what does it matter? They say precisely what the psalmist wants to say: *You cared for us, and brought us into safe pasture. You planted us and made us fruitful. But now look at us. We are scattered and bereft. We have been cut down and yanked up by the roots.*

The psalmist is speaking for all of Israel, and for all of us as well. When what seems like the perfect plan of God is thwarted, when the pruning of our lives cuts at living tissue, when the tears we shed come again and again without warning, we can make the psalmist's refrain our own mantra of prayer: *Restore us, O God. Turn things around—turn us around—so that we can see the light of your face once again. Then, and only then, will we be saved.*

FROM THE FATHERS

"O God of hosts, restore us to our own; smile on us, and we shall find deliverance." For wherever the soul of a person may turn, unless it turns to you, it clasps only to itself. Even if it clings to things of beauty, if their beauty is outside God and outside the soul, it only clings to sorrow.

Augustine

I am not actually in danger of losing my life, Father,
  but sometimes it feels like I am losing my life as I know it . . .
    and, as I have come to love it.
"Save me, Lord," is all Peter had time to pray,
  when the stormy sea engulfed him,
  when it looked like everything was over.
He and this psalmist had a lot in common.
Both of them saw their worlds coming to an end.
And both of them called out to you.
  Will you hear my voice, too?

42

Tuesday of Holy Week
PSALM 130

Out of the depths I cry to thee, O LORD!
Lord, hear my voice!

v. 1

PSALM 130 (ONE OF THE SEVEN PENITENTIAL PSALMS*)
is the testimony of a sufferer—the prayer of one who knows
the inward grief and desperation brought on by one's own
sin. *De profundis*—"out of the deep" (Ps. 130:1, BCP)—evokes the
chaotic and lethal waters before creation, or of the Red Sea, or
of the Sea of Galilee. (See Ps. 69:1–2; Gen. 1:1–2; Exod. 15:5;
Matt. 14:30.) The psalmist cannot feel more in danger or further
removed from God.

The lamentation addresses God as "Lord," the Hebrew name
meaning "sovereign" or "master." It is the personal name of Israel's
God, the name of the One who miraculously delivered them from
their oppression in Egypt by his own mighty right hand. Even by
calling out this exalted name, the psalmist becomes acutely aware
of the *depths* to which sin lowers the human soul. Verse 3 aptly ren-
ders the Hebrew, which uses the deepest and most inward of Old

---

* The Penitential Psalms, so-called since the time of Augustine, are 6, 32, 38,
  51, 102, 130, 143.

Testament words for sin, *iniquity*, which refers to the human heart's confounding propensity to actively seek out ways that separate us from God.

The psalmist feels himself to be drowning under the weight of such offense against God, utterly terrified that if the Lord should take permanent notice of his wrongdoing, his life will be swallowed up altogether. Out of the depths of that profound sense of helplessness—we might say, "from the bottom of his heart"—the psalmist cries out to his God. He cries out in hope because, while he knows that God is holy and just, he also knows that "with the LORD there is mercy, and with him is plenteous redemption" (Ps. 130:7, BCP). And so he "fleeth unto the Lord" (6, BCP), looking for God's salvation with intense expectation, like one who awaits the coming dawn. Anyone who has impatiently waited for the rising of the sun after an endless night of sleeplessness knows something of the ache in the poet's heart.

The psalmist's longing does not go unfulfilled, and for this reason he now has a testimony to share with his listeners. "O Israel, trust in the Lord . . . he *shall* redeem Israel from all his sins" (7–8, BCP, emphasis added). Matching the intensity of his need, there is now an equally profound sense of confidence in his declaration, for the psalmist himself has been saved from deadly waters by the outstretched arm of God's forgiveness. He is a living witness, again, to the God who is "rich in mercy" (Eph. 2:4).

FROM THE FATHERS

We cannot put limitations on the mercy of God or fix limits to times. With him there is no delaying of pardon when the conversion is genuine, as the Spirit of God says through the prophet . . . "Because with the Lord there is mercy; and with him plentiful redemption."

Leo the Great

How many times have I called out to you for mercy, Father?
And how many times have you been faithful in answering?
　　Too many for me to count—only you know.
Your mercy is my food.
It is the air I breathe and the water I drink.
It is my companion all my days.
Without it,
　　I am lost.
With it,
　　I am always home.

43

Wednesday of Holy Week
PSALM 102

Thou changest [the earth and the heavens] like raiment,
and they pass away;
but thou art the same, and thy years have no end.

vv. 26–27

T HOUGH THE AUTHOR OF PSALM 102 IS ANONYMOUS to us, the rather detailed superscription tells us something of his situation: "A prayer of one afflicted, when he is faint and pours out his complaint before the LORD." The psalmist's lamentation is not resolved by some sudden intervention of God. However, his words take on a note of hope and assurance as he contemplates the changelessness of God and the purposes of God that, while too deep to be fully comprehended, are nevertheless motivated by love and faithfulness.

The poem may be divided into three parts. In verses 1 through 11, the psalmist makes his cry for help. He is burdened by an outpoured list of complaints: he suffers from the uncertainties and transience of life ("my days pass away like smoke"); he is sick ("my bones cleave to my flesh"); he is lonely ("I am . . . like an owl of the waste places"); he is persecuted ("all the day my enemies taunt me"); he cannot stop crying ("mingle tears with my drink"); and, above all else, he is afraid that God has deserted him ("thou hast taken me up and thrown me away"). Smoke, bones, withering grass, vultures, eating ashes moistened with tears, thrown away like trash, as fleeting as an evening shadow—the psalmist draws upon all this imagery to describe a condition of utmost despair. This is a Jeremiah voice if there ever was one.

Verse 12 introduces the second section of the psalm (verses 12 through 22), beginning with the words, "But thou, O LORD." These are the words upon which hinge any change of heart or condition. Until this point the psalmist has been speaking only of himself—I this; I that; I the other thing. "But *thou*, O Lord," he now declares emphatically, and the verses that follow lay out the clear contrast between human vicissitude and weakness, and divine unchangeableness and omnipotence. Jerusalem and the temple lay in ruins, their stones scattered and the dust of their walls blowing in the wind. Still, God will act to heal and restore his people. He hears and answers the prayers of those who are troubled. His ways with Zion are a sign of how God meets the needs of all who turn to him and will surely rebuild promises from the rubble of ruined dreams.

The final section of the psalm (verses 23 through 28) brings the first two sections into one. Behind the inconsistencies of human life stands a consistently faithful God. This is more than a matter of contrasts; the psalmist entrusts his frailty to God because he knows that the unchangeable God of eternity is actually *behind* and *within* the changeful lot of his condition. The writer to the Hebrews hears these verses addressed to Christ, the one who is the same yesterday, today, and forever (see Heb. 1:10–12 and 13:8). God is at work and, in contrast to the lament of his opening lines, the psalmist concludes by giving witness with an unshakable faith in an unshakable God.

FROM THE FATHERS

"You are always the same, and your years will never end." Hold most firmly and never doubt that the Holy Trinity, the only true God, is eternal and unchangeable.

Fulgentius of Ruspe

Father, you know well that there are many uncertainties in my life.
And I am the last one to see the next change coming.
But there are no surprises with you . . . no "caught off guard" moments.
Staying with you is my best and only hope for peace.

44

Holy Thursday

PSALM 64

Hide me from the secret plots of the wicked.

v. 2

T HE AUTHOR OF PSALM 64 IS THE VICTIM OF A vicious plot. He looks to God for protection, describes the success of God's intervention and, in the end, rejoices in the Lord who has saved him.

Hide me, he prays, *from the gathering together of evildoers—the wicked, those who are making their secret plans to harm me.* The weaponry chosen by his persecutors includes the sharpest sword that can be wielded against the human soul and the most pointed arrow that can pierce through a human heart: the cutting and poisonous words of a lying tongue. Another psalm says similarly: "Why do you boast, O mighty man, of mischief done against the godly? All the day you are plotting destruction. Your tongue is like a sharp razor, you worker of treachery. You love evil more than good, and lying more than speaking the truth. You love all words that devour, O deceitful tongue" (Ps. 52:1–4).

It looks at first as if the psalmist's adversaries use these weapons with impunity. The wicked have no fear of reprisal as they shoot their fiery darts at the righteous man. They act as if their actions go unseen. They seem to be having their destructive way with no consequences. *But*—once again the entire direction of the psalm turns upon this single little word: *"But* God shall suddenly shoot at them with a swift arrow" (Ps. 64:7, BCP). At *them.* While the psalmist may be helpless to defend himself against the onslaught of his assailants, God's hand is never weakened. This is why vengeance is always to be left to God alone. "Vengeance is *mine*," says the Lord (Rom. 12:19; Heb. 10:30, emphasis added). The psalmist changes from victim to witness as he watches his enemies defeated by their own devices—"their own tongues shall make them fall" (8, BCP). Their lies catch up with them.

In his Rule, and following a long-standing custom of the Western Church, St. Benedict appointed Psalm 64 to be prayed on Wednesdays (*Rule of Benedict*, 13.6), the day of the week in which the religious authorities of the time hatched their plot "to arrest Jesus by stealth and kill him" (Matt. 26:4). Their tool would be the poisoned soul of one of Jesus's own disciples, whose betrayal-laced kiss on Thursday would set their "cunningly conceived plot" (Ps. 64:6) into motion. But, the devil, the chief among all deceivers, was destined to be caught in his own snare. What the psalmist knows, what all people of faith know, is that behind the failure of the cruel and unjust enemy is the saving work of God who alone is just and righteous. The joy and gladness with which the psalmist completes his song is not simply because his enemies got what they deserved, but because he and all who have seen it know that deliverance is something which "God alone has done."

FROM THE FATHERS

For no one who believes that he has at hand a strong helper is frightened by any of those who attempt to throw him into confusion.

Basil the Great

I know, Lord, that your enemy and mine—the enemy of all that is good—
  cunningly plots and schemes for my destruction;
    just as he plotted for yours.
So, if I stay with you—you are my hiding place—
  not only am I in good company,
    but I am in safe keeping.

45

Good Friday

PSALM 69

But as for me, my prayer is to thee, O LORD.
At an acceptable time, O God,
in the abundance of thy steadfast love answer me.

v. 13

PSALM 69 IS AMONG THE MOST OFT-QUOTED PSALMS in the New Testament. For example: verse 4 is found in John 15:25; verse 9 in John 2:17 and Romans 15:3; verses 22 and 23 in Romans 11:9–10; and verse 25 is found in Acts 1:20. A Christian reading of the psalm has traditionally understood these words in connection with the Lord's suffering and death; and its companion is Psalm 22:1, "My God, my God, why hast thou forsaken me?"

Christians have always found in the Psalter references to the life, death, and resurrection of Christ. Jesus himself is recorded as saying to his disciples: "These are my words which I spoke to you, while I was still with you, that everything written about me in the law of Moses and the prophets *and the psalms* must be fulfilled" (Lk. 24:44). In the case of Psalm 69, the things "written about the Lord" are found in the poet's description of his despair, of his sufferings at the hand of others, and of his confidence that God will once again raise him up.

The psalmist moves through a number of phases in his lament. He begins by describing his dreadful condition—despite his own faithfulness to God, he sinks in deep mire, depleted of strength. He then makes his complaint and his petition for help—hear me, O God, and "rescue me from sinking in the mire" (Ps. 69:13, 14). Just as he has been caught in the snare, he hopes that his enemies will fall into the very snares they set for others. Finally, he declares his trust in the Lord, and his confidence that others, too, will know God's goodness as they witness his own deliverance. "Let the oppressed see it," he writes, "and be glad" (32).

It is a wondrous and mysterious journey that is traversed by the poet, as he makes his way from desolation to praise, from ruin to restoration. This is the pathway of all God's saints, and we see its trail again and again throughout the Bible. It is none other than the way of the cross—and, thus, the way of resurrection.

FROM THE FATHERS

It was said with reference to Christ's passion that the waves of the sea rose mightily against him. He freely yielded himself to the storm for our sakes, fulfilling the prophecy: "I came into the depth of the sea, and the tempest overwhelmed me." . . . He did not use his power to quell the raging hearts and stop the mouths of the furious mob, but he bore it with patience. They did to him whatever they wanted, because "he became obedient to death, even death on a cross" (Phil. 2:8).

Augustine

The way of your Cross, Lord,
> *is the way you have called me to follow.*
Today, I pray for courage,
> *for perseverance,*
> *and even for some zeal.*
May these all be my companions,
> *as I make my way to Zion.*

46

Holy Saturday
PSALM 24

Lift up your heads, O gates!
and be lifted up, O ancient doors!
that the King of glory may come in.

v. 9

THE FESTIVE NATURE OF PSALM 24 IS ESTABLISHED by the declaration made in the very opening verses: *everything* is the Lord's. There is not a single thing in all heaven or earth that does not "belong" to God, not so much in the sense of ownership, but in the sense of origin. God reigns over all because he is the source of all. "He himself gives to all men life and breath and everything," wrote the apostle Paul (Acts 17:25). "In him we live and move and have our being" (Acts 17:28). No wonder the Septuagint (the oldest of several ancient translations of the Hebrew Scriptures into Greek) directs that Psalm 24 be used "for the first day of the week" in celebration of the first day of creation.

There is a confident assurance that comes from knowing God's sovereignty over all things, both seen and unseen. We come to

God in prayer because we believe that we live our entire lives under his watchful care, and that nothing occurs outside the realm of his truth and faithfulness. This, says the psalmist, is why we seek the face of the God of Jacob with humility and integrity. Those who would approach his "holy place" must know that he cannot be fooled by appearances (Ps. 24:4).

The last verses of the psalm are an almost playful dialogue between one group of worshipers standing outside the temple door and another group standing inside: *Open the doors! / For whom are we to open them? / For the King of glory! / Who is the King of glory? / You know who he is—the Lord God Almighty!* Like the opening verses of Psalm 105 (see #23), it is possible this song was composed in connection with David's triumphant entry into Jerusalem with the ark of the covenant (see 1 Chr. 15:16–23), or at least for the anniversary of such a jubilant event. It is not hard to understand, therefore, why the psalm eventually made its way into the liturgy for the dedication of churches, where the back-and-forth interchange takes place between bishop and congregation; and on Palm Sunday, when Jesus's triumphal entry into Jerusalem is celebrated; and on Ascension, when he is welcomed through the gates of heaven.

However, the dialogue is anything but playful in another setting for which the psalm traditionally has been used: Holy Saturday. On this day, it is imagined that Jesus approaches the gates of hell (1 Pet. 3:18–19). Christian art pictures the crucified Christ—the King of Glory—standing upon the splintered doors with the devil crushed beneath, reaching out to release from captivity those who are imprisoned in the shadow of death.

Jerusalem, Palm Sunday, Ascension, or Holy Saturday: the God into whose presence we long to enter is the same God who comes to the door of *our* hearts and bids us open.

FROM THE FATHERS

The sun was darkened on the day of our redemption; hell lost its right to us, and we were enrolled in heaven. The eternal gates were lifted up that the King of glory, the Lord of might, might enter in, and human kind, born of the earth and destined for hell, was purchased for heaven.

Tertullian

> *Lord, you open the gates of Paradise for me,*
> > *gates that I could not open myself,*
> > *gates that were closed and bolted*
> > > *on the day of our parents' expulsion.*
> *Your birth and life and death and rebirth,*
> > *together make the combination that unlocks the door,*
> > > *unbars the way, undoes the exile.*
> *You have opened heaven's heart for me—*
> > *how can I refuse you entry into my own?*

47

Easter Sunday
PSALM 98

O sing to the LORD a new song,
for he has done marvelous things!

v. 1

PSALM 98 IS A NEAR COUSIN TO PSALM 96. BOTH psalms call for renewed praise (a "new song") to be offered in the house of the Lord, and both psalms recruit elements of nature to join in the festivities. Psalm 98 also adds to the chorus of sounds a lyre (harp), trumpets, and a horn. All of these instruments, and more (see Psalm 150), were played regularly in the temple.

The horn—literally the "shofar," or ram's horn—was used especially to announce the arrival of the Sabbath and the beginning of all the chief festivals, meaning that this psalm was probably written in honor of one of the grand annual celebrations.*

The reason for the rejoicing is explained, though without naming the specific occasion, in verse 1: "His right hand and his holy arm have gotten [the Lord] victory." Clearly there has been a

---

* A shofar is painted in the fresco at each of the four interior corners of the monastery church here at the Community of Jesus, a visual reminder of the "call to worship" that compels us each day to gather from the "four corners" of our community.

battle of some sort between "the house of Israel" and her enemies, a conflict in which God personally intervened to save his people. This is why the poet speaks of God's "right hand" and "holy arm."

These are images depicting an ever-present God who does not shrink from reaching deep into the lives of his people and getting involved. Whenever these words are used in the Bible, they speak of a God who makes, feeds, supports, rules, leads, blesses, upholds, and rescues. The God and Father of Israel is not one who leaves his children to their own devices, with only themselves to depend upon.

The church knows God's right hand and holy arm as the incarnation, life, death, and resurrection of his mercy and truth: the Son of God himself, and Savior of the world. Psalm 98 praises a God who does not send hired mercenaries, but comes himself to fight for and save his people. His victory will be known from shore to shore (Ps. 98:3), wherever the Sun of righteousness rises in splendor and triumph. Today, let all the strains of praise blend into one supreme new song: *Alleluia, Christ is risen!*

FROM THE FATHERS

"All the earth sing joyfully to God," says [the Lord], and by this command he imposes his shepherdly control over all the earth. The resounding trumpet draws the soldier forth to war; just so does the sweetness of this jubilant call invite the sheep to pasture. How fitting it was to mitigate the din of fighting by shepherdly kindness, in order that such gentle grace might save the nations.

Peter Chrysologus

Father, someday all the earth will be as one voice,
proclaiming your glory and praising your name.
Until that day—
and so I will be ready to sing a truly new song—
I want my heart to learn to sing in tune with heaven.

Who Are the Church Fathers Quoted in This Book?

AMBROSE (ca. 339–Good Friday, 397), **bishop of Milan**

As the son of a Praetorian Prefect in Gaul (modern France), Ambrose embarked on a civil career that eventually took him to Milan, where he served as governor of that region. When the bishop died, Ambrose was pressed by the Milanese people to become the new bishop, even though at the time he was only a *professed* Christian, not yet baptized or ordained. He is considered one of the original four doctors of the Western Church (together with Augustine, Jerome, and Gregory the Great), and for his contribution to the early growth of Christian hymns, he has been called the "Father of Liturgical Hymnody."

ATHANASIUS (ca. 295–373), **bishop of Alexandria**

Athanasius, who was born and raised in Alexandria and served there as a deacon, was made bishop by the popular acclaim of the city's Christians. Despite such initial support, the theological and political controversies of his time forced Athanasius into exile a total of five times. This probably worked to the overall benefit of the church, however, for it was during his years away that Athanasius did the bulk of his writing. He is considered one of the four doctors of the Eastern Church (together with the three hierarchs: Basil the Great, Gregory of Nazianzus, and John Chrysostom).

AUGUSTINE (354–430), bishop of Hippo

One of the most distinguished and influential theologians of the Christian church, Augustine came to faith only after first rejecting the Christian influence of his mother and spending his early years philosophically and morally wandering. Still, he was a seeker, and after a renewed reading of the Scriptures (especially the letters of Paul) and the *Life of St. Antony* (written by Athanasius), and hearing the sermons of Ambrose, Augustine was baptized on Easter in 387. After spending some time as a monk (he would later write a rule for community life), he was ordained a priest, and later made bishop of Hippo in 395.

BASIL THE GREAT (ca. 330–379), bishop of Caesarea

Basil's early attraction to monasticism and the ascetic life was redirected, though never entirely lost, when he was ordained a priest and ultimately made a bishop. His considerable energies were put into pastoral care, service to the poor, theological disputation, and writing, all of which earned him the title of "Great" even before he died. His monastic *Rule* is to the East what the *Rule of St. Benedict* is to the West. As bishop, he preached twice a day, and it is from those many sermons that his *Homilies on the Psalms* have been taken.

CAESARIUS OF ARLES (ca. 470–542), bishop of Arles

As a teenager, Caesarius began his path to Christian ministry when he started theological education and soon after entered the monastery of Lérins in Gaul. Illness, brought on by his severe asceticism, led Caesarius to a different monastery, outside nearby Arles, where he recovered and served for a short time as abbot. It was not long before he was made bishop of Arles, where he served for forty years. Almost 250 of his sermons appear in written form, among them his teachings on the Psalms.

CASSIODORUS (ca. 485–ca. 580), Roman statesman and church scholar

Flavius Magnus Aurelius Cassiodorus was a Roman statesman in one of the most turbulent periods of the Christian West. His life may be divided into two distinct periods: his early political years, when in various capacities he served the Ostrogothic kings in Italy; and his later scholarly monastic years, when he served the church, founded a monastery, and promoted the monastic disciplines of study and manuscript copying. His monumental *Expositio Psalmorum* (which took him more than ten years to write) is a complete commentary on the Psalms.

DESERT FATHERS

The earliest Christian monks were the fourth- and fifth-century hermits and cenobites (those living in communities) who lived in the wildernesses of Egypt, Sinai, Syria, and Palestine. What we know about them comes largely from the collections of their "Sayings"—thousands of proverbs and stories passed down orally at first, and eventually organized and recorded in Greek. Most of the sayings are words of teaching and inspiration given by elder monks to their young disciples, for whom "Father, give me a word" was the most commonly used formula for seeking such instruction.

EUSEBIUS OF CAESAREA (ca. 260–ca. 339), bishop of Caesarea and church historian

A controversial figure in the theological disputes of his time, Eusebius is nevertheless celebrated in both the East and West as the "Father of Church History." He is the author of many writings, the best known of which is his *Ecclesiastical History* in which he traces (through ten volumes!) the history of Christianity from the time of the apostles down to his own day. Though history was his favored topic, Eusebius also wrote on biblical topics, including a series of commentaries on the Psalms.

FULGENTIUS (ca. 467–533), bishop of Ruspe

Born into a family of Roman senatorial rank, Fulgentius seemed destined to a life of civil service. But at the age of twenty-two, after reading a sermon by Augustine on Psalm 36, on the transitory nature of this earthly life, Fulgentius left his home and family to become a monk. His reputation as a spiritual guide and as a wise administrator drew the attention of others and, in 507, he was made bishop of Ruspe (in North Africa). In addition to his pastoral duties, he devoted time to study and writing, drawing especially on Augustine, Ambrose, and Leo the Great to contribute his own treatises defending theological orthodoxy, promoting asceticism, and discussing spiritual principles.

GREGORY OF NYSSA (ca. 335–ca. 395), bishop of Nyssa
Gregory of Nazianzus, Basil the Great, and this Gregory (who was Basil's younger brother) make up the three great fourth-century leaders of Christian orthodoxy known as the Cappadocian Fathers. (Cappadocia is now central Turkey.) Gregory abandoned an early academic career in favor of joining a monastery founded by his brother. When he became bishop of Nyssa, the two vocations merged in his work as a theologian. Particularly in his later life he became known as a gifted preacher, and his homilies on the Lord's Prayer, the Beatitudes, and the Psalms are still being read today.

HILARY OF POITIERS (ca. 315–ca. 367), bishop of Poitiers
Born and raised in Poitiers (in what is now central southwestern France), Hilary did not become a Christian until around age thirty, after a long period of studying the Bible. A few years later he was made bishop of his hometown, where he served as a vigorous teacher and defender of orthodox belief amid the theological conflicts of his day. His most famous work, *On the Trinity*, was written largely as an educational tool for the people of his churches. In the last years of his life, he wrote a commentary on fifty-eight psalms in which he argued that the only way to interpret the Psalms was in light of the life, death, resurrection, and coming again of Jesus Christ.

ISAAC OF NINEVEH (died ca. 700), monastic writer
Little is recorded of Isaac's life. Also known as "Isaac the Syrian," he was originally from Qatar, where he became a Christian and

a monk. Sometime around 675 he was made bishop of Nineveh, but after only five months in office, he withdrew to pursue his monastic vocation, first as a hermit and then as a member of a community in the mountains of what is now southwest Iran. Most of his works—which include prayers, essays on ascetic spirituality, and numerous homilies—were written during the closing years of his life.

JEROME (ca. 345–420), biblical scholar

Born Eusebius Hieronymus, Jerome's early Christian life was spent living the ascetic life with a group of friends in the Roman city of Aquileia. From there he set out for Palestine in 374, but settled for a time as a hermit in the Syrian desert (where he learned Hebrew so that he could better study the Scriptures). He was ordained a priest, worked for a time in Constantinople and in Rome, and finally settled in Bethlehem, where he founded a monastery for men, living by himself in a cave near the traditional birthplace of Jesus. While known especially for his Latin translation of the Bible (the Vulgate), Jerome is also the author of numerous commentaries on the Scriptures, including notes and homilies on the Psalms.

JOHN CASSIAN (ca. 360–ca. 430), monk and spiritual writer

John Cassian was born in present-day Romania. As a young man, he traveled with his friend Germanus to Bethlehem, where he joined a monastery. From there he spent years making extended visits to the hermitages and monasteries of the Egyptian desert, which became the subject of his two most influential writings, the *Institutes* and the *Conferences*. The first is an exposition of monastic and spiritual principles; the second is Cassian's reconstruction of his many dialogues with Egyptian abbots. Written primarily for the instruction of two monasteries that he founded in Marseilles (one for men, one for women), the volumes were influential in the development of monasticism in the West.

JOHN CHRYSOSTOM (ca. 347–407), bishop of Constantinople

John was born in Antioch and, until he was made bishop of Constantinople in 398, he spent his entire life and ministry in and around this important city. He was baptized at eighteen and, after some years learning and living the life of an ascetic, which included time as a hermit in the mountains outside the city, he was ordained and appointed the preacher for the cathedral. His skill and dedication to this vocation earned him the name Chrysostom ("golden mouth"). From those and subsequent years, we have a large collection of his homilies on the various festivals of the church, the Gospels, the Acts of the Apostles, Paul's letters, and the Psalms.

JOHN OF DAMASCUS (ca. 657–ca. 749), monk and theologian

Born into a prosperous family in Damascus, John was educated in both Greek and Arabic, and studied science and theology under the tutelage of a monk from Sicily. It is thought that he served for a time as an administrator in the court of the Muslim caliph, but soon resigned his post in order to become a monk, be ordained, and join the monastery of St. Sabas near Jerusalem. His many writings have influenced the theology of both East and West. (Thomas Aquinas read his works thoroughly.) He is known for his defense of the use of icons in the church and for his contributions to the Byzantine liturgy, including a number of hymns (some in modern translation, e.g., "Come, ye faithful, raise the strain").

LEO THE GREAT (died 461), bishop of Rome

One of only two bishops of Rome to be honored with the title "Great" (Gregory), Leo served the Church in a time of political, social, and theological upheaval. He was only a deacon when, in 440, he was elected pope. He immediately set to strengthening the role of the papacy, advocating the primacy of the bishop of Rome and increasing papal influence in the West. He was equally known for his compassion and courage, never more evident than when he convinced Attila the Hun to withdraw his attacking forces from the Italian peninsula. Together with other writings, he left almost one hundred sermons, covering the entire liturgical year.

NICETAS (died ca. 414), bishop of Remesiana

Remesiana was a Roman city built on a military road between Belgrade and Constantinople, in what is today southeast Serbia. As such, the city bridged East and West, and its bishop, Nicetas, was in conversation in both directions with church leaders and theologians. Little is known of his early life, but he has left us with a collection of writings that indicates his dedication to Christian education (catechesis); his love of hymnody (he is likely the author of the enduring Latin hymn *Te Deum laudamus*); and his interest in the liturgy (he promoted the use of music during worship and urged that psalms be sung during the night vigil before Sunday morning Eucharist.)

PALLADIUS (ca. 363–ca. 431), bishop and monastic historian

Palladius was born in Galatia (the central region of modern Turkey) and as a young man travelled to Egypt to live among the well-known monks and hermits of that day, the so-called Desert Fathers. There he became a disciple of Evagrius of Pontus, one of the monastic tradition's most influential theologians. When he returned to Asia Minor in 400, he was made a bishop and became a close friend and supporter of John Chrysostom, with whom he also shared the trouble of periodic exile. While away from the duties of his office, Palladius authored a history of the early desert monks, which became the leading source for understanding the beginnings of monasticism.

PETER CHRYSOLOGUS (ca. 380–450), bishop of Ravenna

In the time of Peter Chrysologus, Ravenna's most illustrious bishop, the city was the capital of the Western Roman Empire and as such the center of much secular and ecclesiastical activity. Under the patronage of the emperor's mother, Galla Placidia, Chrysologus embarked on a number of building projects designed to further the church's mission in the region and to strengthen its role within the Empire. His sermons, though simple and short, were known to be theologically rich and very direct in their delivery. They earned him the title "Doctor of Homilies" and as many as 176 of them have survived.

TERTULLIAN (ca. 160–ca. 220), writer and apologist

Most of what we know of Tertullian's life is from the writings of Jerome and Eusebius, though his works give us more insight into this great Christian author. He was the son of a Roman centurion, born and raised in the city of Carthage (in North Africa). There he received an extensive education before becoming a Christian and beginning his writing career. His works focused on theology, asceticism, and apologetics (refuting accusations against Christianity and defending the church's beliefs). He was the first significant Christian author to write in Latin, earning for himself the title "Father of Latin Theology."

THEODORET (ca. 393–ca. 460), bishop of Cyrrhus

A native of Antioch, Theodoret was raised a Christian and educated in monastery schools. He became a monk himself before being elected bishop of Cyrrhus in 423 (the ruins of the city now sit at the border between Syria and Turkey). While his diocese was only about forty square miles in size, he recorded that it was home to almost 800 churches. In addition to his service to those churches, which included building bridges and public buildings, the young bishop went on to become one of the most prolific writers of the Greek church. His works include histories of the church and the monks of Syria, and a series of commentaries on various books of the Bible, including the Psalms.

References for Quotations from the Church Fathers

Unless otherwise notated, all of the quotations from the church fathers are taken with permission from:

Psalms 1–50 edited by Craig Blaising and Carmen Harden. Copyright © 2008 by the Institute of Classical Christian Studies (ICCS), Thomas C. Oden, Craig A. Blaising, and Carmen S. Hardin. Used by permission of InterVarsity Press, P.O. Box 1400, Downers Grove, IL 60515, USA. www. ivpress.com

Psalms 51–150 edited by Quentin Wesselschmidt. Copyright © 2007 by the Institute of Classical Christian Studies (ICCS), Thomas C. Oden and Quentin Wesselschmidt. Used by permission of InterVarsity Press, P.O. Box 1400, Downers Grove, IL 60515, USA. www.ivpress.com

1   Taken from *Psalms 51–150*, page 342.

2   Taken from *Psalms 51–150*, page 415.

3   Taken from *Psalms 51–150*, page 366.

4   Taken from *Psalms 1–50*, page 2.

5   Taken from *Psalms 1–50*, page 12.

6   Taken from *Psalms 1–50*, page 95.

7   Taken from *Psalms 1–50*, page 63.

8   Augustine, *Exposition on Psalm* 136.

9   Taken from *Psalms 1–50*, page 351.

10   Taken from *Psalms 1–50*, pages 158, 159.

11   Taken from *Psalms 51–150*, page 385.

12   Taken from *Psalms 51–150*, page 410.

13   Taken from *Psalms 1–50*, page 323.

14   Taken from *Psalms 1–50*, page 273.

15   Taken from *Psalms 1–50*, page 289.

16   Taken from *Psalms 1–50*, page 389.

17   Taken from *Psalms 51–150*, page 16–17.

18   Taken from *Psalms 51–150*, page 49.

19   Taken from *Psalms 1–50*, page 206.

20   Taken from *Psalms 51–150*, page 91.

21   Taken from *Psalms 51–150*, page 125.

22   Irene Nowell, OSB, *Pleading, Cursing, and Praising: Conversing with God through the Psalms* (Collegeville, MN: Liturgical Press, 2013), 33.

23   Taken from *Psalms 51–150*, page 248.

24   Taken from *Psalms 51–150*, page 328.

25   Taken from *Psalms 51–150*, page 110.

26   Taken from *Psalms 51–150*, page 375.

27   Taken from *Psalms 51–150*, page 87–88.

28   Taken from *Psalms 51–150*, page 191.

29   Taken from *Psalms 51–150*, page 339.

30   Taken from *Psalms 51–150*, page 285.

31   Taken from *Psalms 51–150*, page 399.

32   Taken from *Psalms 1–50*, page 37.

33   Taken from *Psalms 51–150*, page 177.

34   Taken from *Psalms 1–50*, page 105.

35   Taken from *Psalms 1–50*, page 135–36.

36   Taken from *Psalms 1–50*, page 225.

37 Taken from *Psalms 51–150*, page 25.

38 Taken from *Psalms 1–50*, page 216.

39 Taken from *Psalms 51–150*, page 123.

40 Taken from *Psalms 51–150*, page 310.

41 Taken from *Psalms 51–150*, page 139.

42 Taken from *Psalms 51–150*, page 361.

43 Taken from *Psalms 51–150*, page 215.

44 Taken from *Psalms 51–150*, page 56.

45 Taken from *Psalms 51–150*, page 76.

46 Taken from *Psalms 1–50*, page 188.

47 Taken from *Psalms 51–150*, page 199.

Notes

1   Athanasius, "The Letter to Marcellinus," in *Athanasius*, trans. and
ed. Robert C. Gregg (New York: Paulist Press 1980), 126.

2   John Calvin, quoted in William L. Holladay, *The Psalms Through
Three Thousand Years: Prayerbook of a Cloud of Witnesses* (Minneapolis:
Fortress Press, 1993), 196.

3   Irene Nowell, OSB, *Pleading, Cursing, and Praising: Conversing with God
through the Psalms* (Collegeville, MN: Liturgical Press, 2013), 31.

4   Augustine, *Exposition of the Psalms, 99–120*, trans. Maria Boulding
(Hyde Park, NY: New City Press, 2003), 525.

5   Martin Luther, preface to the *Wittenberg Edition of Luther's German
Writings*, quoted in John Piper, *Taste and See* (Colorado Springs,
CO: Multnomah, 2016), 280.

6   John Cassian, *John Cassian: The Conferences*, trans. Boniface Ramsey, OP
(New York: Paulist Press, 1997), 382.

7   John Calvin, *John Calvin, Heart Aflame: Daily Readings from Calvin on
the Psalms* (Phillipsburg, NJ: P&R Publishing, 1999), 304.

ABOUT PARACLETE PRESS

Who We Are

Paraclete Press is a publisher of books, recordings, and DVDs on Christian spirituality. Our publishing represents a full expression of Christian belief and practice—from Catholic to Evangelical, from Protestant to Orthodox.

We are the publishing arm of the Community of Jesus, an ecumenical monastic community in the Benedictine tradition. As such, we are uniquely positioned in the marketplace without connection to a large corporation and with informal relationships to many branches and denominations of faith.

What We Are Doing

Paraclete Press Books | Paraclete publishes books that show the richness and depth of what it means to be Christian. Although Benedictine spirituality is at the heart of all that we do, we publish books that reflect the Christian experience across many cultures, time periods, and houses of worship. We publish books that nourish the vibrant life of the church and its people.

We have several different series, including the best-selling Paraclete Essentials and Paraclete Giants series of classic texts in contemporary English; Voices from the Monastery—men and women monastics writing about living a spiritual life today; award-winning poetry; best-selling gift books for children on the occasions of baptism and first communion; and the Active Prayer Series that brings creativity and liveliness to any life of prayer.

Mount Tabor Books | Paraclete's newest series, Mount Tabor Books, focuses on the arts and literature as well as liturgical worship and spirituality, and was created in conjunction with the Mount Tabor Ecumenical Centre for Art and Spirituality in Barga, Italy.

Paraclete Recordings | From Gregorian chant to contemporary American choral works, our recordings celebrate the best of sacred choral music composed through the centuries that create a space for heaven and earth to intersect. Paraclete Recordings is the record label representing the internationally acclaimed choir Gloriæ Dei Cantores, praised for their "rapt and fathomless spiritual intensity" by *American Record Guide*; the Gloriæ Dei Cantores Schola, specializing in the study and performance of Gregorian chant; and the other instrumental artists of the Arts Empowering Life Foundation.

Paraclete Press is also privileged to be the exclusive North American distributor of the recordings of the Monastic Choir of St. Peter's Abbey in Solesmes, France, long considered to be a leading authority on Gregorian chant.

Paraclete Video | Our DVDs offer spiritual help, healing, and biblical guidance for a broad range of life issues including grief and loss, marriage, forgiveness, facing death, bullying, addictions, Alzheimer's, and spiritual formation.

Learn more about us at our website:
www.paracletepress.com or phone us
toll-free at 1.800.451.5006

SCAN
TO
READ
MORE

Also Available from Paraclete Press. . .

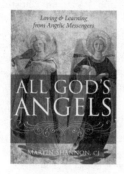

All God's Angels:
Loving & Learning from Angelic Messengers
Martin Shannon, CJ

ISBN 978-1-612-61774-9 | $19.99 | Paperback

There is an entire realm of divine activity that human eyes cannot perceive—at least not without God's unveiling grace. The angels belong to this invisible world. The author pulls back the veil between heaven and earth with biblical stories, meditations, and sacred art on the role of heavenly messengers and their work in our lives. Angels are servants of love, doing God's bidding with a theology of burning love. God seeks out his servants, and once he has our attention, he draws us closer, long enough for the sparks of his glory to reach us and ignite a flame in our own souls.

This book is a series of reflections on the angelic visitations that are recorded in the Bible, in both the Old and New Testaments. Each entry includes a Scripture reading, an artistic image, a reflection and questions for consideration or discussion.

Between Midnight and Dawn:
A Literary Guide to Prayer for Lent, Holy Week and Eastertide
Sarah Arthur

ISBN 978-1-612-61663-6 | $18.99 | Paperback

Experience the liturgical seasons of Lent, Holy Week, and Eastertide in the company of poets and novelists from across the centuries.

This third literary guide compiled by Sarah Arthur completes the church calendar with daily and weekly readings for Lent and Easter from classic and contemporary literature. New voices join well-loved classics by Dostoevsky, Rossetti, and Eliot. Light in the darkness, illuminating the soul. This rich anthology will draw you deeper into God's presence through the medium of the imagination.

PRAISE FOR SARAH ARTHUR'S LITERARY GUIDES:

"A rich feast."—Lauren F. Winner, author of *Still*

"I may just be a bit smitten with this book."—Ann Voskamp, author of *One Thousand Gifts*

Available through your local bookseller or through Paraclete Press:
www.paracletepress.com; 1-800-451-5006